UNDERSTANDING LITURGY

Making Sense of the Rites and Rituals of the Catholic Church

CHARLIE DISPENZIERI, M.A.P.T.

ISBN 978-1-0980-1083-6 (paperback)
ISBN 978-1-0980-1084-3 (digital)

Christian Faith Publishing, Inc.
832 Park Avenue
Meadville, PA 16335
www.christianfaithpublishing.com

Printed in the United States of America

To Charlie Gardner, Fr. Rick Ginther, David Groeller, Fr. Pat Beidelman, and Fr. Julian Peters, OSB. I cannot even begin to express how grateful I am to these liturgical mentors who have shared their wisdom, time, and patience with me as they helped form me into the liturgist I am today. Their willingness to guide and support me has had a massive influence on my life and on those whom God has allowed me to serve throughout the years.

To all those family, friends, clergy, and parishioners who have supported me throughout the years in liturgical ministry.

All of these people have enriched my life, and I trust this book will serve you in understanding and appreciating the rites and rituals of the Catholic Church.

CONTENTS

THE MASS

THE SACRAMENTS OF THE CATHOLIC CHURCH

THE LITURGICAL YEAR

Liturgical Rites

INTRODUCTION

When people talk about liturgy, they are willing to share their opinions about how Mass should be celebrated, the length of the service, the type of music that should be sung, and if the homily was good or bad. People really do get animated about liturgy! *Understanding Liturgy* is written for all who want to learn more about the Catholic liturgy. There is much to learn, and in the following pages we will explore many facets of what makes up the church's rites and rituals.

This book is not a comprehensive text on every aspect of liturgical theology. It encompasses topics that have come from questions I have received from parishioners and clergy. The chapters will give you a starting point for more reflection on each individual topic, and help you gain a better understanding of sacramental and pastoral liturgy without too much in-depth theology. *Understanding Liturgy* encompasses specific aspects of celebrating the liturgy and the ritualistic components of the rites.

It could also serve as the introductory text for a course on Liturgy, a resource for adult education programs at either the parish or diocesan level, and could be used for formation and enrichment for liturgical minister training. *Understanding Liturgy* is also suited as a resource for parish liturgy committees.

Liturgy is the communal prayer of the church. It is first and foremost the work of God, celebrated together as the body of Christ assembled in his church. As ritual prayer, it happens over and over again, so much so that sometimes we don't understand fully the power of the ritual being celebrated. We pray together as the people of God, coming together to be changed, transformed by the grace of the Holy Spirit and the presence of Christ. We come to church to celebrate liturgy with full, conscious, and active participation during our prayer. When we leave church, we should be changed; transformed to be of service to the world and to each other because we are called to build up the kingdom of God.

The vision of this text is to be a vehicle for liturgical formation for all Catholics and those who are interested in learning about the Catholic faith and its prayer. *Understanding Liturgy* is written to help all appreciate the Catholic liturgy and to enter into it deeper, not just as an obligation, but as a part of the believer's life, helping them become as Pope Francis teaches "a missionary disciple." It is my hope that you will come away with a better appreciation for the heritage we have as Catholics—a tradition we hold dear to our hearts—and a better understanding of what we do and why we do it. I pray you will gain a greater appreciation for liturgical rites and rituals and experience God's presence in the prayer of the Church.

Charlie Dispenzieri

Liturgical Art and Environment

The church is the proper place for the liturgical prayer of the parish community, especially the celebration of the Eucharist on Sunday. Churches, therefore, must be places "suited to sacred celebrations," "dignified," and beautiful.

—*Rite of Dedication of a Church and an Altar: chapter 2, no. 3*

Incense

The Church teaches that incense is an expression of reverence and prayer. The Bible records many instances when people used incense to enhance prayer. Aaron presented a bull as a sin offering for himself, placing two handfuls of sweet incense on the fire (Leviticus 16:11–13). Zechariah offered incense at the altar of the Lord (Luke 1:9). We pray in Psalm 141, "Let my prayer be incense before you; uplifted hands an evening offering." In John's vision, an angel with a golden censor offered a great quantity of incense with the prayers of all the saints on the golden altar before the throne of God (Revelation 8:3).

Incense was used at Mass starting around the sixth century. By the twelfth century, the rules for the use of incense became more elaborate during the time following the Council of Trent.

Incense is a sacramental sign that can be seen, smelled, and even heard. The *General Instruction of the Roman Missal* (GIRM) teaches us, "Thurfication or incensation is an expression of reverence and of prayer, as signified in Sacred Scripture" (GIRM, #276). In the liturgy, incense directs our attention to the holy, to the presence of God.

Incense may be used during the entrance procession; at the beginning of Mass, to incense the cross and altar; at the procession before the Gospel and the proclamation of the Gospel itself; during the preparation of the altar and gifts, after the bread and wine have been placed on the altar, to incense the offerings, the cross, and the altar, as well as the priest and the people; and at the elevation of the host and chalice after the Consecration.

Since incense is a sign of reverence to honor people or sacred objects, Holy Mother Church gives us instruction on how each incensation should be carried out. Three swings of the thurible or censer (the vessel where the incense is burned over lighted charcoal) are used to incense the most Blessed Sacrament, a relic of the holy cross and images of the Lord expressed for public veneration, the offerings for the sacrifice of the Mass, the altar cross, the books of the Gospels, the paschal candle, the priest, and the people. Two swings of the censer are used to incense relics and images of the saints. The altar is incensed with single swings of the thurible. Before and after each of these incensations, a profound bow (deep bow of the waist) is made to the person or object being incensed except for the altar and offerings.

Incense is also used during the dedication of a church. The incensation of the main body of the church indicates that the dedication makes it a house of prayer. But the People of God are incensed first, for they are the living temple in which each faithful member is a spiritual altar (The Order of the Dedication of a Church, #17).

Incense is usually a combination of organic materials, which when burned release a fragrant aroma. These consist of aromatic gums from trees (frankincense and myrrh fall into this category), some woods, barks, seeds, fruits, and flowers can be burned as incense also. There are dozens of incense blends available including hypo-allergenic incense blends. Some of the most popular are Holy Night Incense and Pontifical (Three Kings) Incense.

When I was working with the Office of Worship in the Archdiocese of Indianapolis, a monk from St. Meinrad Abbey taught me how to make my own mixture of incense to be used during each liturgical season. He also mentored me on the importance of creating a proper mixture associated with each liturgical rite. For example, during the entrance procession we need a long period of smoke, during Eucharistic benediction a shorter burst of smoke is better.

Powder-like or sawdust-like incense produces aroma immediately and burns for a brief time. Grains usually burn longer after a slower start, very large grains or pellets often take time to produce smoke, but they burn for a very long time with a rich fragrance. The mixture of the incense used is of great importance!

Brother Howard's liturgical wisdom still inspires me today to create a different fragrance of incense for each liturgical season. Incense truly does help us lift our prayers to God. Incense adds a sense of solemnity to the Mass. The visual imagery of the smoke and the smell remind us of the transcendence of the holy sacrifice of the Mass, which links heaven and earth and allows us to enter into the presence of God.

Liturgical Colors

In our everyday life we associate certain colors with particular celebrations, such as red, white, and blue for the Fourth of July and the color of our favorite sports teams. In our religious life, colors also have a meaning. Liturgically they suggest a mystery or feast, or the significance of the occasion for which Mass is celebrated. Since the altar linens are always white, the liturgical color refers to vestments and the environment.

The early church used only one liturgical color—white—symbolizing new life attained in Christ. In those days, colored clothing was so expensive that only the wealthy could afford it. Not until twelfth-century Jerusalem, when dyes were more commonplace, did liturgical colors start to become law. In the thirteenth century we find the guidelines for the liturgical colors that we basically follow today: white for festive days and saints, red for martyrs and the Holy Spirit, green for ordinary time, and violet for the penitential seasons.

The list of vestment and environment colors for Masses and for other liturgies is found in the *General Instruction of the Roman Missal* (#346–#347). This document states that traditional usage should be retained. Here is a brief summary of what the missal states about liturgical colors:

The color white is used in the offices and Masses during Easter time and Christmas time; on the Solemnity of the Most Holy Trinity; and on celebrations of the Lord other than of his Passion, celebrations of the Blessed Virgin Mary, of the Holy Angels, and of Saints who were not Martyrs; on the Solemnities of All Saints and of the Nativity of St. John the Baptist; and on the Feasts of St. John the Evangelist, of the Chair of St. Peter, and of the Conversion of St. Paul.

The color red is used on Palm Sunday, Good Friday, on Pentecost Sunday, on celebrations of the Lord's Passion, on the "birthday" feast days of Apostles and Evangelists, and on celebrations of Martyr Saints. The color green is used in the offices and Masses of ordinary time. The color violet is used in Advent and Lent. The color rose may be used on the third Sunday of Advent and on the fourth Sunday of Lent.

The variety of liturgical color is meant to give an outward expression to the specific character of the mysteries of faith being celebrated during the course of a liturgical year.

LITURGICAL VESTMENTS

The liturgical vestments at Mass worn by lay people, priests, deacons, and bishops express the rich diversity of the ministries we have in the Catholic Church. The *General Instruction of the Roman Missal* (GIRM) is very clear on the importance of this distinctive vesture: "In the Church, which is the Body of Christ, not all members have the same function. This diversity of offices is shown outwardly in the celebration of the Eucharist by the diversity of sacred vestments, which must therefore be a sign of the function proper to each minister" (GIRM # 335).

The vestment we commonly see worn as an outer garment by altar servers and those who serve as a master of ceremonies is known as the *alb*. This is really a baptismal garment and is white in color. Bishops, priests, and deacons also wear albs, but as their inmost vestment layer. The *cincture* is an embellishment to the alb, and functions as a belt. The *Funeral Pall*, a large piece of fabric, is placed on the coffin when we celebrate a funeral Mass. It covers the entire coffin and serves as a reminder of our white baptismal garment.

Vestments proper to the ordained include the stole, dalmatic, and chasuble. The *stole* is a scarf like vestment, which is the mark of ordination. Deacons wear it over the left shoulder, drawn across the chest and back toward the lower right side. Other ordained ministers wear it around the neck, so it hangs down evenly in front. The *dalmatic* is the outer vestment of the deacon worn over the alb and stole. It has sleeves which makes it look distinctively different from the chasuble, the outer vestment worn by priests. The *General Instruction of the Roman Missal* (GIRM) is very brief concerning the chasuble. The GIRM states, "The vestment proper to the priest Celebrant at Mass and during other sacred actions directly connected to Mass is the chasuble, unless otherwise indicated, over the alb and stole"

(GIRM # 337). The *chasuble* is a circular garment with an opening for the head. Prior to vesting, an *amice* is tied around the waist. An amice is a square piece of white linen with two long pieces of fabric and serves to cover a person's street clothes.

The *cope* is a long semicircular cloak, open in the front and reaching down to the heels of the person wearing it. There is a clasp near the neckline, which holds the vestment around the shoulders. This cope is used outside of Mass for such celebrations as Liturgy of the Hours, Eucharistic Exposition, and outdoor processions. The *humeral veil* comes from the Latin word for shoulder. This large, scarf-like veil has a clasp with a chain to keep it secured on the person. The humeral veil is worn by a priest or deacon during Eucharist Exposition, Eucharistic processions, and while holding the monstrance for the blessing during benediction.

At any liturgical celebration, the liturgical vestments worn by a bishop are the same as those worn by a priest. Bishops may also wear a dalmatic between the stole and chasuble. In addition to the liturgical vestments, a bishop will also wear certain insignia or clothing. The Ceremonial of Bishops (CB) teaches, "The pontifical insignia belonging to the bishop are: the ring, pastoral staff, and the miter and the pallium, if he is entitled to use it" (CB, #57).

The *ring* which the bishop wears expresses the fidelity he has to the local church. The symbol of the bishop's pastoral office, used at more solemn celebrations is the crozier (from the Latin meaning crook) or *pastoral staff*. The bishop will carry it or hold it during processions, when he listens to the gospel reading, and at other times called for in the rite he is celebrating.

The *miter* is worn at most liturgies when the bishop presides as a symbol of his liturgical presidency. Normally, the bishop wears the miter when he is seated, when he greets people, during a solemn blessing over the people, when he is conferring a sacrament, and at other times designated in the Ceremonial of Bishops. The miter consists of two pieces of heavy fabric forming a circle at the bottom that rises to two peaks at the top. At the back of the miter are two pieces of fabric that extend downward.

The bishop wears a *zucchetto* (skull cap) at almost every liturgy. During liturgies when the bishop is not wearing the zucchetto, it rests on the cathedra or the priest celebrant's chair.

A bishop also wears a *pectoral cross*. It is a cross on a chain that rests near his chest. It is worn under the chasuble, dalmatic, or cope. The *pallium* is a narrow band of white wool, worn over the chasuble. It is worn only by an archbishop, that is, a bishop of dioceses designated as the metropolitan center with certain jurisdiction over neighboring dioceses. Each pallium is given by the pope to archbishops as a sign of the metropolitan's communion with Rome. They are woven from white lamb's wool shorn from two lambs blessed by the pope on the Feast of St. Agnes.

As ceremonial clothing, liturgical vestments express the nature of the occasion. They also clearly define the respective role of each participant as well as adding symbolism.

THE ALTAR

The word "altar" came to be used in the early Christian church to designate the table on which was placed the bread and wine for Eucharist. The Greek language speaks of the altar as "the table of sacrifice." Saint Paul writes about the "table of the Lord" (1 Corinthians 10:21), and it is at a table that Jesus foretells his death, giving us the sacrificial gift that we will celebrate in his memory until we assemble at the banquet in heaven.

The altar, then, is a symbol of Christ in the midst of the assembly of believers, a table dedicated for both the sacrifice and the paschal banquet. Originally the altar was a simple free-standing table for the first few centuries of Christian worship, but it was soon affected by a changing theology of Christian worship. This theology created a liturgy performed largely by the clergy, and the placing of the altar on the rear wall of the apse meant that the altar was no longer the table of the assembly. It was primarily the resting place for the bread and wine, the missal, candles, flowers, and later, the tabernacle.

The Second Vatican Council revised the norms relating to the altar and used the earliest tradition of the church as its guide. The United States Bishops teach us in the document "Built of Living Stones, Art, Architecture, and Worship," "The altar is the center of thanksgiving that the Eucharist accomplishes and the point around which the other rites are in some manner arrayed. Since the Church teaches that the altar is Christ, its composition should reflect the nobility, beauty, strength, and simplicity of the One it represents" (BLS, #56).

During the dedication of an altar, the bishop anoints the altar with Sacred Chrism. This action "makes the altar a symbol of Christ, who before all others, is and is called "The Anointed One" (Rite of Dedication of a Church and an Altar, #22a). The altar then should be treated as a piece of furniture that honors the holy action that occurs there. It is not just a table that can be moved to the back wall of our sanctuary, just to give us more space.

The altar is the table on which the sacrifice of the cross is perpetuated in mystery throughout the ages. It is the table where we gather to give thanks to God and to receive the Body and Blood of Christ. The altar stands then as a worthy symbol of Christ and a holy table where God's people are nourished for their pilgrimage.

THE AMBRY

An ambry is the cabinet where the holy oils are stored. Every church has one, though many people don't know what it's called or even where to find its location.

> The consecrated oil of chrism for initiation, ordination, and the dedication of churches, as well as the blessed oils of the sick and of catechumens, are traditionally housed in a special place called an ambry or repository. These oils consecrated or blessed by the bishop at the Mass of Chrism deserve the special care of the community to which they have been entrusted. (*Built of Living Stones*, 117)

There are three glass vessels of oils in the ambry. One contains the Oil for Anointing the Sick (OI), the Oil for Anointing Catechumens (OC), and Sacred Chrism (SC) for baptism, confirmation, priesthood, and the consecration of altars and walls.

The basis for all three oils is ordinary virgin olive oil. Sacred Chrism also contains balsam. It tends to be a little darker in color and has a sweet, perfume smell. The oil that was not used from the previous year is burned in the Easter Vigil fire. In this way the ambry is always replenished with fresh oil every year.

The shape and size of an ambry varies from parish to parish. The ambry should be made of a suitable material with a design that is appropriate for its sacred contents. Holy Mother Church reminds us of the importance of placing the holy oils in a simple, dignified, and secure location "After a priest anoints the sick, he is instructed to return the extra oil to a place where it is reverently kept" (Pastoral Care of the Sick, no 22).

Because the holy oils are used in the sacraments of initiation to anoint before and after baptism as well as in the sacrament of Confirmation, they are housed near the baptismal font and serve to remind us of our own entrance into the Church through these sacraments.

It makes sense to place the parish ambry in a location that allows it to be seen. By keeping these holy oils in dignified vessels and displaying them in an honorable case, our worshipping community can better regard the significance of the sacraments when we gather to celebrate our faith.

THE LITURGICAL ENVIRONMENT

The primary reason Catholic churches are built is to celebrate the Eucharist. Of course we use the church for many other occasions as well, including funerals, weddings, and private prayer. The primary design and liturgical environment décor of a church depends on what is needed for Sunday Mass and the liturgical year. The building gets its name from the people who gather in the church. The liturgical document *Built of Living Stones: Art Architecture and Worship* (BLS) teaches, "The church building is both the house of God on earth (domus Dei) and a house fit for prayers of the saints (domus ecclesiae). Such as house of prayer must be expressive of the presence of God and suited for the celebration of the sacrifice of Christ, as well as reflective of the community that celebrates there" (BLS# 16).

The church building allows the community a place to meet God. In our Catholic tradition, we celebrate the sacraments in church because they are the prime ways we encounter God as a community. A wide range of features is encompassed in the scope of church environment. Some examples are the Sanctuary, the Nave, various chapels, the Baptismal Font area including the ambry, Reconciliation Rooms, vestments, vessels, the sacristies, Holy Water Stoups, Common and devotional areas and also many types of linens and fabric.

The liturgical environment must be prepared appropriately to serve the worship occasion. Each aspect of the church building should show that there is a dignity in that sacred place. What is important should look important; the celebration of the sacraments and all our worship is distinct and significant. Our worship space and all associated spaces should be seen as worthy and honored. This is also true for the liturgical furniture and liturgical books used. Any materials used for sacred furnishings, according to the *General Instruction of the Roman Missal* (GIRM) # 326, must be "considered to be noble, are durable, and are well suited for sacred use." Liturgical books particularly the lectionary and Book of the Gospel, are intended for the proclamation of the Word of God, so they need to be "truly worthy, dignified, and beautiful" (GIRM # 349).

The liturgical space must be able to facilitate the action. Placing flowers in front of the altar, for example, will make it very difficult to approach, reverence, and incense the table of the Eucharist. The active participation of the worshipping community must always be considered. This requires that people can both see and hear each other, so sight lines and appropriate room size is important. A small chapel will help facilitate intimate prayer for 50 people, but those same folks would feel lost in a space designed for 900 people. The size of the space also dictates the dimensions of the objects needed for that space. You may have a vase of flowers on your kitchen table which look beautiful, but that same vase would be dwarfed in a large church and would not be appropriate.

Religious art stems from our faith, the doctrines of the church, and the lives of the saints. Sacred images should lead the faithful toward the mysteries of faith celebrated in that space. The tradition of decorating the sacred spaces of our church for each liturgical season and feasts heightens the awareness of the festive, penitential, or solemn nature of the season. *Built of Living Stones* reminds us that, "Human minds and hearts are stimulated by the sounds, sights, and fragrances of liturgical seasons, which combine to create powerful, lasting impressions of the rich and abundant graces unique to each of the seasons" (BLS, #123).

Much consideration also goes into the vestments worn by the clergy. "The purpose of a variety in the color of the sacred vestments is to give effective expression even outwardly to the specific character of the mysteries of faith being celebrated and to a sense of Christian life's passage through the course of the liturgical year" (GIRM, #345). All vessels used for liturgical celebrations are also set apart from those of everyday use.

Liturgists speak about the importance of noble simplicity, which simply stated is all about avoiding clutter and showing the dignity of the entire scared space. Liturgy is formative—clutter or disarray, tables in the Commons that are not set up neatly, or dead or dying flowers speak volumes about a lack of realization of where we are and the reverence that is required in sacred space. We need to always remember, we celebrate in the house of God, a sacred temple and it should look the part.

All materials used in church, especially flowers and candles, should be real, as GIRM # 292 instructs us, "For church appointments there should be a concern for genuineness of materials." Lighting and sound reinforcement is also part of the liturgical environment. Everyone needs to hear the prayers prayed by the presider, the proclamation of sacred Scripture, the Universal Prayer, the music ministry, and each other.

Liturgical art and architecture reflect and announce the presence of the God who calls the community to worship and invite believers to raise their minds and hearts to the one who is the source of all beauty and truth (BLS, #44). Care always needs to be taken to be sure our liturgical environment in all its many forms complement and do not detract from any liturgical celebration.

Feasts and Solemnities

In the cycle of the Liturgical year, as she celebrates the mystery of Christ, the Church also venerates with a particular love the Blessed Mother of God, Mary, and proposes to the devotion of the faithful the Memorials of the Martyrs and other Saints. Those Saints who have universal importance are celebrated throughout the whole Church and are inscribed in the calendar for celebration. *(Universal Norms on The Liturgical Year and The Calendar: no. 8–9)*

ALL SAINTS' DAY AND ALL SOULS' DAY

All Saints' Day is a holy day of obligation. This day is dedicated to all the saints of the church, those known and known to all who are enjoying the glory of heaven. From the first centuries after Christ, Christians who died a martyr's death were considered saints, living in the eternal presence of God forever. Every year, on the anniversary of the martyrs' deaths, Christians would visit their tombs and also celebrate the Holy Eucharist. This practice grew throughout the centuries to include remembering other Christians on the days they also died. Pope Gregory IV, in the ninth century, designated November 1 as the day to remember all the saints living in God's presence.

The beatitudes are proclaimed from the Gospel according to Matthew every year on All Saints' Day. These beautiful passages have Jesus on the mountain teaching us about what it means to be blessed. If that were not enough, the Master then tells us about the reward given to those who are proclaimed blessed. All the saints in heaven are blessed, and now their reward is enjoying the heavenly kingdom. For us still here on earth the message is clear—we must live these beatitudes today right where we are, as followers of Jesus. Our reward then will also be the heavenly kingdom.

Throughout the Preface (the prayer before the Holy, Holy, Holy) for this great solemnity, we hear the theology concerning all those who have attained heaven already: The priest prays from the Roman Missal (RM), "For today by your gift we celebrate the festival of your city, the heavenly Jerusalem, our mother, where the great array of our brothers and sisters already gives you eternal praise" (RM, Preface: The glory of Jerusalem, our mother). Further into that same Preface, we hear how we are like pilgrims, moving toward that same heavenly kingdom: "Towards her, we eagerly hasten as pilgrims advancing by faith, rejoicing in the glory bestowed upon those exalted members of the Church through whom you give us, in our frailty, both strength and good example" (RM, Preface: The glory of Jerusalem, our mother).

The Commemoration of the Faithful Departed or All Souls' Day is celebrated following the solemnity of All Saints' Day. Having commemorated all the blessed who enjoy the face of God in their death, we turn our thoughts to the other souls who await the fullness of God's glory. Celebrating The Commemoration of the Faithful Departed originated early in the Middle Ages in monastic communities as an annual day of prayer for the dead. All Souls' Day began to be celebrated throughout the church after the tenth century. The texts we use to celebrate this Mass are drawn from the collection we use at our funeral liturgies. These readings express faith in the Communion of Saints and our need to pray especially for those who have died and await their final joy in heaven.

All Souls' Day is celebrated on November 2. Let's be clear, the church remembers all who have died not only on this particular day, but at every Mass throughout the year. The Universal Prayer (also called The Prayer of the Faithful or General Intercessions) will always contain a petition for those who have died in the faith of Christ.

In the Eucharistic Prayer of every Mass, we also pray for those who have died. This remembrance occurs in the section after we sing the Mystery of Faith acclamation. The "*Memento etiam*" section prays for those Christians who have died. We pray in the Roman Canon (Eucharistic Prayer I), "Remember also, Lord, your servants, who have gone before us with the sign of faith and rest in the sleep of peace. Grant them, O Lord we pray, and all who sleep in Christ, a place of refreshment, light and peace" (Roman Missal, Eucharistic Prayer I). It is interesting to note that those mentioned in this section of the prayer are called servants, just as when we remembered all the living earlier in the Eucharistic Prayer. This servant connection begins at our baptism and continues throughout our life. The Opening Prayer of a Funeral Mass echoes this when the priest prays,

"Grant that your servant who has gone to his/her rest in Christ, may share in the joy of his/her resurrection" (Order of Christian Funerals).

In The Prayer after Communion on All Souls' Day, the priest continues this theme when he prays, "Grant we pray, O Lord that your departed servants, for whom we have celebrated this paschal Sacrament, may pass over to a dwelling place of light and peace" (Roman Missal). On this day we pray that God will have mercy on them and grant them the vision of blessedness for which they longed.

The feast of All Souls' celebrates our union with the church in every place and beyond all time and space.

Eternal rest grant unto them, O Lord, and let perpetual light shine upon them.

Requiem aeternam dona eis Domine: et lux perpetua luceat eis.

CHRISTMAS PROCLAMATION

The announcement of the Solemnity of the Nativity of the Lord from the Roman Martyrology draws upon Sacred Scripture to declare in a formal way the birth of Christ. It begins with creation and relates the birth of the Lord to the major events and personages of sacred and secular history. The particular events contained in the announcement help pastorally to situate the birth of Jesus in the context of salvation history.

The text for the nativity of our Lord Jesus Christ is proclaimed on Christmas Eve during the celebration of the Liturgy of the Hours. Most people, though, will hear it proclaimed before the beginning of Christmas Mass during the night, which we call traditionally Midnight Mass.

Here is the Christmas Proclamation from Appendix I of the *Roman Missal, Third Edition:*

The Twenty-fifth Day of December,
when ages beyond number had run their course
from the creation of the world,
when God in the beginning created heaven and earth,
and formed man in his own likeness;
when century upon century had passed
since the Almighty set his bow in the clouds after the Great Flood,
as a sign of covenant and peace;
in the twenty-first century since Abraham, our father in faith,
came out of Ur of the Chaldees;
in the thirteenth century since the People
of Israel were led by Moses
in the Exodus from Egypt;
around the thousandth year since David was anointed King;

in the sixty-fifth week of the prophecy of Daniel;
in the one hundred and ninety-fourth Olympiad;
in the year seven hundred and fifty-two
since the foundation of the City of Rome;
in the forty-second year of the reign of Caesar Octavian Augustus,
the whole world being at peace, Jesus Christ,
eternal God and Son of the eternal Father,
desiring to consecrate the world by his most loving presence,
was conceived by the Holy Spirit,
and when nine months had passed since his conception,
was born of the Virgin Mary in Bethlehem of Judah,
and was made man:
The Nativity of Our Lord Jesus Christ according to the flesh.

While the announcement of the Solemnity of the Nativity of the Lord from the Roman Martyrology (Christmas Proclamation) liturgically occurs at the Mass at Midnight, The Blessing of the Manger scene usually occurs at the Vigil Mass of Christmas Eve. The *Book of Blessings* teaches us that as early as the fourth century representations of the nativity of the Lord were painted as wall decorations.

The current representation and for many people, the custom of displaying figures depicting the birth of Jesus Christ owes its origin to St. Francis of Assisi, who made the Christmas crèche or manger scene for Christmas Eve about 800 years ago. St. Francis was concerned that the meaning of Christmas was becoming lost as most people were more focused with the ritual of gift giving than they were of the true message of Christmas. He was determined to remind people what Christmas is really about, so he created the world's first known nativity scene to help tell his people of the real nativity story.

This first manger scene was created in a cave and near Greccio, Italy, and involved real people and animals, making it also a living nativity scene. It is very appropriate to bless the manger scene you have set up in your home. It may be blessed by a parent or another family member.

Here is the blessing of a manger or nativity scene from the *Book of Blessings* # 1558:

All make the sign of the cross. The leader then prays the following prayer with hands joined:

God of every nation and people,
from the very beginning of creation
you have made manifest your love:
when our need for a Savior was great
you sent your Son to be born of the Virgin Mary.
To our lives he brings joy and peace,
justice, mercy, and love.
Lord,
bless all who look upon this manger;
may it remind us of the humble birth of Jesus,
and raise our thoughts to him,
who is God-with-us and Savior of all,
and who lives and reigns forever and ever.
All respond: Amen

May you and your loved ones experience the peace, love, and joy of Christ!

Epiphany Proclamation

In ancient times before calendars were common, most people did not know the dates for the upcoming liturgical year, so on Epiphany Sunday, the upcoming dates were "proclaimed" after the gospel so people would know when the church would celebrate them.

The celebration of Easter can fall anywhere between March 22 and April 25 as the Sunday after the "Paschal Full Moon" determines when Easter is liturgically set. Because the date of Easter varies from year to year, some other important feasts of the church such as Ash Wednesday and The Ascension of the Lord will also have moveable dates from year to year. As we know, other liturgical feasts such as Christmas and the Immaculate Conception are fixed on our liturgical calendars as well as in our hearts and minds.

Although calendars now give the date of Easter and the other feasts in the liturgical year for many years in advance, the Epiphany Proclamation still has value. It is a reminder of the centrality of the resurrection of the Lord in the liturgical year and the importance of the great mysteries of faith which are celebrated each year.

The singing of the Epiphany Proclamation is a wonderful practice during our celebration on the Solemnity of the Epiphany of the Lord since it brings to the forefront the importance that the rhythm of the liturgical year should hold in our life as a Catholic.

Here is an example of The Announcement of Easter and the Moveable Feasts also known as The Epiphany Proclamation.

Know, dear brethren (brothers and sisters),
that, as we have rejoiced at the Nativity of our Lord Jesus Christ,
so by leave of God's mercy

we announce to you also the joy of his Resurrection,
who is our Savior.
On the sixth day of March will fall Ash Wednesday,
and the beginning of the fast of the most sacred Lenten season.
On the twenty-first day of April you will celebrate with joy Easter Day,
the Paschal feast of our Lord Jesus Christ.
On the second day of June will be the Ascension of our Lord Jesus Christ.
On the ninth day of June, the feast of Pentecost.
On the twenty-third day of June the feast of the Most Holy Body and Blood of Christ.
On the first day of December, the First Sunday of the Advent of our Lord Jesus Christ, to whom is honor and glory for ever and ever. Amen.

Hopefully, this proclamation will also serve as a springboard for each one of us to engage in ongoing catechesis on the liturgical year. Here is a very brief overview of the liturgical year to get us started:

The liturgical year is made up of six seasons, each with a different emphasis on the Paschal Mystery (the life, death, and resurrection) of Christ:

Advent—the four weeks of preparation before the celebration of Jesus' birth
Christmas Time—the church recalls the nativity of Jesus Christ and his manifestation to the peoples of the world
Lent—is a six-week period of penance before Easter

Sacred Paschal Triduum—the holiest "Three Days" of the church's year, where the Christian people recall the suffering, death, and resurrection of Jesus

Easter Time—the fifty days of joyful celebration of the Lord's resurrection from the dead and his sending forth of the Holy Spirit

Ordinary Time—which is really divided into two sections (one span of four to eight weeks after Christmas and another lasting about six months after the Easter season), wherein we, the faithful, consider the fullness of Jesus's teachings and works among his people.

May the mystery of Christ, unfolded through the cycle of the liturgical year, touch us, so we may meditate on his life, death, and resurrection every day of our lives. Amen!

Our Lord Jesus Christ, the King of the Universe

The official name for the last Sunday of ordinary time is the Solemnity of Our Lord Jesus Christ, King of the Universe. Pope Pius XI established this solemnity in 1925.

This day was created to remind us to celebrate an identity of Jesus rather than an aspect of his life. This feast should foster awareness to us of Christ's dominion over all people and to establish peace to all nations.

The goal is not to think of a variety of images of Jesus dressed in kingly robes. This feast celebrates Christ's kingship in an altogether non-worldly way. The Preface of this Mass (the prayer before the Holy, Holy) reminds us that Jesus was anointed by the Father with the oil of gladness as the eternal priest and king of all creation. He offered his life on the altar of the cross and redeemed the human race by this one perfect sacrifice of peace.

The opening prayer names God as the one whose will it is to restore all things in Jesus, who is the king of the universe. This prayer has strong ramifications for each one of us. If we are to actually proclaim Christ as king, then we must be part of the unity and peace his kingdom will establish. In The Prayer after Communion the church continues this theme when the celebrant prays, "Having received the food of immortality, we ask, O Lord, that, glorying in obedience to the commands of Christ, the King of the universe, we may live with him eternally in his heavenly Kingdom" (Roman Missal).

In the gospel according to John, we hear the words of Jesus, "My kingdom does not belong to this world." Jesus pursues not a kingdom here on earth, but rather a heavenly kingdom. The words Jesus use to answer Pilate's question states that he has come from

God the Father to reveal God's truth, not to grab any type of political power or dominion. In other words, Pilate asked political questions, and Jesus took the conversation to the theological level. Jesus admitted to being the king who decided to come into the world to be for it but not of it. This reminds us of God's love and our need to make it known by our word and deed. We are reminded of this through the commissioning we are given at the end of every Mass when the priest or deacon says, "The Mass is ended, go in peace, glorifying the Lord by your life."

This solemnity always falls on the Sunday before the first Sunday of Advent, which is the start of the new liturgical year. The Solemnity of Our Lord Jesus Christ, King of the Universe, celebrates Jesus's role as king over all. This solemnity of Christ the King enables us once again to consider our role in the world and Christ's kingship over us and all creation. However, we must remember that Jesus is king because he is a servant to all. Jesus's kingship is one of power and might, but also humility.

May we always strive to serve others in all we do!

Presentation of the Lord

The Presentation of the Lord involves many aspects of our spiritual life. These include candles, blessings, Christmas, and the church. The Mass of February 2 begins with a blessing of candles that remind us of the memory of the birth of Jesus.

The origins of the feast lie in ancient Jewish custom. On the fortieth day after childbirth, parents brought the infant to the temple to present their child to the Lord and to purify the mother. St. Luke tells us that Joseph and Mary sacrificed two birds for the occasion after the birth of Jesus.

Until the 1960s, we called this day "The Purification of Mary." Since we no longer believe that women who give birth need purification and the true significance of the feast concerns Jesus coming to the Temple, as the Promised One, whose light will shine on the nations, the title of this feast was changed.

If you count up forty days after Christmas, you'll come to February 2. Even though the date for the Presentation still depends on Christmas, it is a feast of ordinary time. If you like to use blessed candles for household prayer throughout the year, bring your candles to church on the Presentation of the Lord and have them blessed.

On the day following this feast, we celebrate the feast of St. Blaise, a bishop and martyr of the early church. Legend has it that he once freed a child from choking, and while imprisoned under persecution he received light from friends who visited his cell with candles. Our church still uses candles from the Presentation of the Lord in the blessing of the faithful's throats on St. Blaise's Day.

Blessed candles in our churches and homes signify the living presence of Christ in our community. With Christ as our light we warm a lost and wintry world.

The Dedication of the Lateran Basilica

St. John Lateran is one of the four major basilicas in Rome, with St. Peter, St. Mary Major, and St. Paul outside the walls. It is unique among the four because it (not St. Peter's) is the cathedral church of the bishop of Rome.

"Lateran" was the name of a Roman family whose land was seized for the Church by the Emperor Constantine. It later became the site of a great basilica dedicated to honor John the Baptist. For many centuries, the old Lateran palace was the residence of popes. It was only after the fourteenth century that the popes actually started to live at the Vatican.

The basilica now has a triple dedication in honor of St. John the Baptist, St. John the Evangelist, and our Lord. It is very interesting to note that in front of the basilica there is an inscription in Latin that says, "This is the mother and head of all churches in the whole world." This reminds us why we celebrate this dedication throughout the universal Church on November 9. We truly are one family, and are led by one shepherd, who is the successor of St. Peter.

When the feast of the Dedication of the Lateran Basilica falls on a Sunday, the readings and prayers for the feast replace those of the Sunday celebration. There is a special preface for the Eucharistic Prayer provided for the day; it's entitled "The Mystery of the Church, the Bride of Christ, and the Temple of the Spirit." Throughout the entire prayer we hear the theology of the feast. This prayer reminds us that every church is a house of prayer. "For in your benevolence you are pleased to dwell in this house of prayer in order to perfect us as the temple of the Holy Spirit, supported by the perpetual help of your grace and resplendent with the glory of a life acceptable to you. Year by year you sanctify the Church, the Bride of Christ, foreshadowed in visible buildings, so that, rejoicing as the mother of countless children, she may be given her place in your heavenly glory" (Roman Missal, Preface, Dedication of the Lateran Basilica). The clergy wear white vestments and a solemn blessing is provided. Although we mark the dedication of a building, more importantly we give thanks for the church itself, God's "chosen" and "faithful" people, who will "build up the heavenly Jerusalem" (Roman Missal, Collect, first option).

The Dedication of the Lateran Basilica is not the only Roman basilica celebrated on the liturgical calendar of the Catholic Church. In addition to the feast of the Lateran Basilica, we also celebrate the memorials of The Dedication of two other basilicas. The first is the Basilica of St. Mary Major, which is celebrated on August 5. The original name of this church was Our Lady of the Snows, and has within its walls relics of the manger in Bethlehem. The Dedication of the Basilicas of Saints Peter and Paul, the two apostles, is celebrated on November 18. We must realize that while we are remembering the church building on these days, it is more about the saints to whom each of these buildings are dedicated.

Let's also remember that the diocesan cathedral's dedication day is important. This day is celebrated in all the parishes of that specific diocese as a memorial each year. On a parish level, the anniversary of the dedication of a local parish church building is celebrated as a solemnity for that parish community. This feast will outrank most of the Sundays in ordinary time. Lastly, the patron of the parish may also be celebrated as a feast. On this day, the "Glory to God" is sung, the dedication candles on the four pillars of the church are lit, and the celebrant wears white vestments.

The Rite for the Dedication of a Church and Altar (RDCA) is a beautiful and solemn liturgy. Throughout that liturgy, we are reminded that it is Christ himself who is the eternal priest, the saving victim, and the altar of sacrifice. The theology of how the church building will function and serve God's holy people is made very clear. The church is the place where the local community (and others) will gather to hear the proclamation of the Sacred Scriptures and celebrate the sacraments, especially the Most Holy Eucharist. This image of the church speaks of its importance as a temple to celebrate the Sacred Mysteries. In the Opening Prayer of the Rite of Dedication of a Church and Altar, the bishop prays, "Lord, fill this place with your presence, and extend your hand to all those who call upon you. May your word here proclaimed and your sacraments here celebrated strengthen the hearts of all the faithful" (RDCA # 52, Opening Prayer).

The celebration of the Dedication of the Lateran Basilica helps in prompting us to remember other dedications for the local and universal Church. The Catholic church is truly one, holy, catholic, and apostolic. When we all celebrate feasts from the General Roman Calendar we show the unity of Christ's body, symbolized in so many church buildings but made present in living assemblies.

LITURGY AND DEVOTION

In her ritual actions, the Church proclaims the Gospel of salvation and announces the Death and Resurrection of Christ. In the Eucharist she celebrates the memorial of his blessed Passion, his glorious Resurrection, and Ascension. The celebration of the Liturgy, however, does not exhaust the Church's divine worship. Authentic forms of popular piety are also fruits of the Holy Spirit and must always be regarded as expressions of the Church's piety. *(Directory on Popular Piety and the Liturgy: no 81–83)*

Blessings

Throughout the liturgical year, the church will bless a variety of ministers, individuals, and objects. These can include lectors, musicians, and altar servers; Mothers and Fathers; an Advent wreath, manger scene, or ashes for our Ash Wednesday celebration. These blessings are scheduled to coincide with a certain aspect of the liturgical calendar such as the feast day of a saint, a seasonal celebration or an event in the life of a parish.

Throughout sacred Scripture, we find how God issued various blessings. In the account of creation, God blessed all the living creatures especially Adam and Eve, telling them to be fertile, to multiply, and to fill the earth (Genesis 1:22, 28). After the flood, God blessed Noah and his sons (Genesis 9:1).

Jesus blessed those he encountered: the little children (Mark 10:13–16) and the Apostles at the Ascension (Luke 24:50–53). He blessed objects: the loaves used to feed the 5,000 (Mark 6:34) and the bread of the Last Supper (Matthew 26:26–30). Since Christ entrusted his saving ministry to the church, it has instituted various blessings for people as well as objects to prompt the faithful to implore God's protection, divine assistance, mercy, faithfulness, and favor.

The celebration of blessings holds a privileged place among all the sacramentals in the Church. Blessings are called "sacramentals" because they prepare us to receive the grace of the sacraments and help us to grow to be more like Christ (Catechism of the Catholic Church, # 1670).

From the grace and power received in the Eucharist, the Church itself becomes a blessing existing in the world (*Book of Blessings*, # 8). The Church as the universal sacrament of salvation continues the work of sanctifying as it gives honor and glory to God the Father.

The Church has many forms of blessings. There are times when blessings praise God; some encourage us to ask for God's protection, still others invite us to ask for God's mercy. When we celebrate a blessing, it's really a time to praise and give glory to God. The blessing should help us become better people.

Blessings are a part of the liturgy of the Church. A communal celebration of a blessing shows the character of liturgical prayer, since those who are present join themselves in mind and heart with the Church. In those cases where the community is not present, the individual should remember they are part of the larger community and in that instance they represent the community. While the blessing is administered on the behalf of an individual it should actually in some way benefit the entire community.

Most people are accustomed to seeing bishops, priests, and deacons blessing objects or persons in the name of the Church. Indeed, "the more a blessing concerns ecclesial and sacramental life, the more is its administration reserved to the ordained ministry," often with the participation of the local parish community gathered in prayer (Catechism of the Catholic Church, #1669).

However, there are other blessings that can be prayed by anyone who has been baptized, "in virtue of the universal priesthood, a dignity they possess because of their baptism and confirmation" (*Book of Blessings*, # 18). The *Book of Blessings*, written by St. Pope John Paul II, is very clear concerning which blessings a lay person may preside over.

The blessings given by laypersons, in non-liturgical circumstances, are exercised because of their special office, such as parents on behalf of their children. The Catechism teaches "every baptized person is called to be a 'blessing' and to bless" (Catechism of the Catholic Church, #1669). In other words, when we gather around the family table, we should bless God and the food he has given us. Parents could bless their children. We should call on God's blessing when someone sneezes.

A typical liturgical communal celebration of a blessing outside of Mass consists of a proclamation of the Word of God, a praise of God's goodness, the petitions for his help, and the actual Prayer of

Blessing. There usually is also an Introductory Rite and a Concluding Rite. Some blessings have a special relationship to the sacraments, so they may be celebrated during Mass. The *Book of Blessings* offers a variety of options for each blessing to allow for pastoral adaptations depending on each individual circumstance.

Blessings help us become more aware of God's presence in our lives. They help to connect our liturgical prayer life in church to our personal life. May we always thank God for all the blessings he has given us! Amen.

Holy Water

When we use holy water it should remind us of our baptism. Holy Mother Church teaches, "Baptism is the door to life and to the kingdom of God" (Rite of Baptism, General Introduction, #3). Baptism is the sacrament by which we are incorporated into the church. It unites us into the Body of Christ. So rich in meaning is the rite, that we first bless its water. We pray that the Holy Spirit will vivify the water, making it fit for its holy purpose.

A priest or deacon may pray the church's water blessing at any time of year, but the blessing of all blessings happens during the Easter Vigil. The water we bless at the Easter Vigil does not last the whole year. Parish priests and deacons will bless water throughout the liturgical year, so holy water from our baptismal font is always available for us. In our Catholic tradition, we also keep holy water at the doors of the church and in all chapels so everyone may have access to it. This holy water is made available to us so we can make the sign of the cross with the water and reminds ourselves that we are a child of God and part of the family of God. When we make the sign of the cross, it should not be rushed since we should reflect upon why we are signing ourselves.

A water blessing and sprinkling rite can replace the Penitential Act on any Sunday (*General Instruction of the Roman Missal*, # 51). The term "Asperges" is the Latin name that was used for the ceremony of sprinkling with holy water at Mass. It comes from verse 9 of Psalm 51, "Cleanse me with hyssop: that I may be pure, wash me, and I will be whiter than snow." During the Easter season is an appropriate time to bless the water at Mass and then continue the sprinkling rite. During this holy season, the prayer of blessing reminds us of the magnitude of God's creation. The celebrant prays, "Lord our God, in your mercy be present to your people's prayers and, for us who recall the wondrous works of creation and the still greater work of redemption, graciously bless this water" (Rite for the Blessing and Sprinkling of Water, # 2). There are also images of water that help grow the crops we consume and water that will refresh our bodies. The priest continues in that same prayer, "For you created water to make the fields fruitful and to cleanse and refresh our bodies." The prayer also takes us throughout a large section of salvation history. With the vessel of water in front of him he continues, "You also made water the instrument of your mercy: for through water you freed your people from slavery and quenched their thirst in the desert…through water, which Christ made holy in the Jordan, you have renewed our corrupted nature in the bath of regeneration" (Rite for the Blessing and Sprinkling of Water, # 2). Throughout the entire prayer, we are reminded of the great things God has done for his people through the use of water.

On those days when the priest walks around sprinkling with water at the beginning of Mass, he's helping us make the connection between that Sunday and Easter, between baptism, faith, and new life. There are many styles and types of vessels that are appropriate for a sprinkling rite. Some churches use the traditional situla (a bucket looking vessel) or a beautiful bowl. The actual sprinkling device could be the traditional aspergillum, branches, or wisps of straw are also suitable.

The water used in the font is constantly replenished. We are very zealous in our care for the water itself. The General Instruction to Christian Initiation #18 and 20 teaches us, "The water used should be pure and clean, both for authentic sacramental symbolism and for hygienic reasons." The font of living water is the heart of both the baptismal area and the community that is born there. In order to enhance its force as a sign, many fonts are designed so it functions as a fountain or stream of running water.

Many parishioners continue the praiseworthy practice of bringing some baptismal (holy) water to their homes. If you decide to follow that practice, then you will able to bless yourself every time you enter your dwelling. Whenever we are sprinkled with holy water or use it in blessing ourselves as we enter the church, a chapel, or our home, we are taking the opportunity to thank God for the gift of being incorporated into the Body of Christ. Sometimes Catholics really don't think about what holy (baptism) water symbolizes, they just dip the finger into the font and make a quick sign of the cross as an automatic gesture. Yet this simple action speaks about our life in faith. Blessing ourselves with holy water gives the faithful an opportunity to ask for God's help to keep them faithful to the Sacrament of Baptism, which they have received in faith.

Inaudible Prayers

Throughout the celebration of every Mass, you will hear the priest pray a variety of prayers. Examples of these include the Eucharistic Prayer, the Orations (Let us pray…), and the Invitation to Communion (Behold the Lamb of God). These are all proclaimed in a clear, loud voice so that all may hear the words of the prayers. Yet there are times also when the priests (and deacons) are praying other prayers at Mass you do not hear. These prayers are said quietly. Throughout the celebration of the Eucharist, the Roman Missal instructs the priest (and deacon) to say certain prayers quietly rather than audibly. These prayers occur before the Gospel, during the preparation of the altar and gifts, and at Communion time.

To understand the function of these prayers, we need to review the way in which Mass first was celebrated. The Mass originated as a public prayer, a dialogue with God by the ministers and the assembly. Eventually as fewer people understood Latin, the participation of the people became less and less until it finally diminished. These inaudible prayers entered the texts of the Mass when the priest was whispering most of them.

The Constitution on the Sacred Liturgy (CSL) teaches, "The Church earnestly desires that all the faithful be led to that full, conscious, and active participation in liturgical celebrations called for by the very nature of the liturgy" (CSL # 14). The Second Vatican Council restored the vocal role of the assembly, leaving only a few prayers to be said quietly by the priest or deacon. Reflecting on these prayers offer us an opportunity to realize the devotion priests and deacons have to the celebration of the Eucharist. Throughout the celebration of the Mass, the ordained have a constant attention to their prayer, which is a model for all of us to follow.

Let's review some of the inaudible prayers that occur at Mass. Whenever a deacon is present at Mass, he proclaims the Gospel. Once the Gospel Acclamation is begun, he approaches the presider and asks in a low voice for the priest's blessing, by saying, "Your blessing, Father." The priest then says in a low voice, "May the Lord be in your heart and on your lips that you may proclaim his Gospel worthily and well, in the name of the Father, and of the Son, and of the Holy Spirit." The deacon signs himself with the sign of the cross and then replies, "Amen."

If, however, a deacon is not present, the priest, bowing to the altar, says quietly, "Cleanse my heart and my lips, Almighty God, that I may worthily proclaim your holy Gospel." After the proclamation of the Gospel, the priest or deacon kisses the book and quietly says, "Through the words of the Gospel may our sins be wiped away."

Several inaudible prayers appear during the preparation of the altar and the gifts. The first prayer prayed quietly (unless the singing of the "Preparation Song" is completed) is a prayer over the gifts which focus on the generosity of God, the produce of the earth, human labor in general, and the Eucharist. The priest takes the paten with the bread and holding it slightly raised says, "Blessed are you, Lord God of all creation, for through your goodness we have received the bread we offer you: fruit of the earth and work of human hands, it will become for us the bread of life."

Following that prayer, the priest or deacon pours a small amount of water into the chalice. The priest or deacon then says, "By the mystery of this water and wine may we come to share in the divinity of Christ, who humbled himself to share in our humanity." There is much antiquity in the ceremony of mixing of water and wine. This preparation appeared in some of the earliest records of the Eucharist. St. Justin the Martyr wrote about this action back in the second century.

The priest next takes the chalice and elevates it slightly as he says in a low voice, "Blessed are you, Lord God of all creation, for through your goodness we have received the wine we offer you: fruit of the vine and work of human hands, it will become our spiritual drink."

Following this, the priest, makes a profound bow and says quietly, "With humble spirit and contrite heart may we be accepted by you, O Lord, and may our sacrifice in your sight this day be pleasing to you, Lord God." At this moment the priest humbly asks God to accept the sacrifice and the people that will be offered. This prayer originated from the story of the three young men in the fiery furnace delivered by Azariah in the Book of Daniel (Daniel 3:39).

Next, the priest, while standing at the side of the altar, washes his hands and quietly quotes Psalm 51, "Wash me, O Lord, from my iniquity and cleanse me from my sins." The washing of his hands shows his desire for interior purification.

Another occasion which calls for a quiet prayer by the presider occurs during the singing of the "Lamb of God." After the priest breaks the large host, he places a small portion in the chalice and says quietly, "May this mingling of the Body and Blood of our Lord Jesus Christ bring eternal life to us who receive it." This action of fractioning part of the host goes back to the time of Pope Innocent. As the bishop of Rome, he sent some of the consecrated bread from his Mass to other churches around the city. The acolytes delivered the particles to the priests who were celebrating Mass in their own church. Before Communion began each of these priests would put that particle from the pope into the chalice. This was a sign of Eucharistic Communion among the churches with the pope. As the Church continued to grow and expand, this practice was impossible to maintain due to the sheer number of churches. While the original reason for the breaking of a small piece of the host was no longer viable, the practice still continues. One meaning we associate today with the priest fractioning a small piece of the host and then placing it into a chalice is the uniting of the Body and Blood of Jesus serving as a sign of the Resurrection.

Following that action, the priest has a choice of two prayers that will help him prepare appropriately so he may fruitfully receive the Body and Blood of the Lord. Both of these prayers have a tremendous richness to them. The first option is "Lord Jesus Christ, Son of the living God, who, by the will of the Father and the work of the Holy Spirit, through your death gave life to the world, free me by this, your most holy Body and Blood, from all my sins and from every evil: keep me always faithful to your commandments, and never let me be parted from you." The second option is "May the receiving of your Body and Blood, Lord Jesus Christ, not bring me to judgment or condemnation, but through your loving mercy be for me protection in mind and body and a healing remedy."

Prior to receiving Holy Communion, all gathered express our unworthiness and pray for healing (Lord, I am not worthy that you should enter under my roof…). The priest then says quietly, "May the body of Christ keep me safe for eternal life" and "May the blood of Christ keep me safe for eternal life." These two texts are relatively late additions to the Mass. They first appeared in the Missal during the Middle Ages.

Following Holy Communion, the particles and droplets of the consecrated bread and wine are collected and consumed by the priest, deacon, or instituted acolyte. While the priest carries out the purification, he says quietly, "What has passed our lips as food, O Lord, may we possess in purity of heart, that what has been given to us in time may be our healing for eternity." The words of this prayer have really not changed since the sixth century.

When the distribution of Communion and the purification is completed, the priest (and the entire worshipping community) prays silently for a time. Holy Mother Church offers us this time of sacred silence so we may appreciate more fully what has just occurred, namely that the eternal Son of God became incarnate and shared himself with us in such an intimate manner.

The *General Instruction of the Roman Missal* (GIRM) teaches, "For the Priest, as the one who presides, expresses prayers in the name of the Church and of the assembled community; but at times he prays only in his own name, asking that he may exercise his ministry with greater attention and devotion. Prayers of this kind, which occur before the reading of the Gospel, at the Preparation of the Gifts, and also before and after the Communion of the Priest, are said quietly" (GIRM # 33). Although these prayers largely go unnoticed, they show the care priests and deacons bring to the celebration of the Mass.

LITURGICAL BOOKS

There are many liturgical books used throughout the celebration of a given liturgy, depending on the actual celebration. Here is a very brief summary of some of the more commonly used liturgical books.

The *Roman Missal* is the book containing the prescribed prayers, chants, and instructions for the celebration of Mass in the Roman Catholic Church. In 2002, Saint John Paul II introduced the "third typical edition" (since the Second Vatican Council) for use in the Church. This is our current version.

The *Lectionary* is composed of the readings and the responsorial psalm assigned for each Mass of the year. Not all of the Bible is included in the *Lectionary*. Individual readings in the *Lectionary* are called pericopes, from a Greek word meaning a "section" or "cutting."

The *Book of the Gospel* contains the Gospel readings that will be proclaimed at Mass. The book includes Gospels for Sunday, solemnities and feasts of the Lord and saints, and seventeen ritual Masses.

The *Rite of Christian Initiation of Adults* (RCIA) contains the rites for the celebration of the sacraments of baptism, confirmation, and Eucharist, and the rites belonging to the catechumenate, such as the Scrutinies we celebrate during Lent.

The *Order of Christian Funerals* contains all the rites the Church celebrates to commend the dead to God's merciful love and asks forgiveness of their sins.

The *Pastoral Care of the Sick: Rites of Anointing and Viaticum* is used by the Church to comfort the sick in time of anxiety, to encourage them to fight against illness, and perhaps to restore them to health.

The *Order for Solemn Exposition of the Holy Eucharist* contains the text and rites for use during Solemn Exposition of the Holy

Eucharist. This ritual book provides several settings for the Liturgy of the Hours and two Eucharistic Services of Prayer and Praise.

The Church has an abundance of other ritual books including the *Liturgy of the Hours* (which is the public, daily prayer of the Church), the *Rite of Marriage*, the *Rite of Penance*, and the *Book of Blessings*, among others.

Throughout the course of an entire year, the Church unfolds the entire mystery of Christ and observes the birthdays of the saints (Universal Norms on the Liturgical Year and the General Roman Calendar, #1). To help us in this area, we use a book called an *Ordo* (Latin for order), which gives information on the liturgy of each day, including the readings, the saints, as well as information on the Liturgy of the Hours. The ordo used is specific to each diocese or religious community.

All liturgical books should always be attractively bound, dignified, and worthy in their condition, since they contain the words of the prayers to be recited or sung and indicate the actions to be performed at a given celebration (*Liturgiam authenticam,* # 120). All these liturgical books help us pray. Since we are truly blessed with a wide variety of prayers for different circumstances, we need an entire library of liturgical ritual books.

LITURGICAL PARTICIPATION

The celebration of Mass is truly an act of the entire worshipping community who gather for worship. This guiding principle occurs throughout the document "The Constitution of the Sacred Liturgy" (CSL). This document of Vatican II states, "Mother Church earnestly desires that all the faithful be led to that full, conscious and active participation in liturgical celebrations which is demanded by the very nature of the liturgy" (CSL, 14).

This active participation was not simply understood as external. The liturgy is more than the words we hear, say, and sing. Liturgy also includes our attitude, our postures, our gestures, our movements, our reflective silence, and our offerings.

The *General Instruction of the Roman Missal* (GIRM) teaches, "The celebration of Mass, as the action of Christ and the people of God arrayed hierarchically, is the center of the whole of Christian life for the Church both universal and local, as well as for each of the faithful individually" (GIRM 16). Each of us has a role in the Mass, since we form a holy people. Through our baptism we are part of the priesthood of Christ, which is the basis for all liturgical ministries.

Bishops and priests are called to act in the liturgy in the very person of Christ, on behalf of his people. In addition to the ordained ministries, some liturgical roles are exercised by lay people. Many times we think these roles only include readers, servers, those who distribute Communion, those who greet us, hand out worship aids, or sing as part of the music ministry. This catalog of roles might give the impression that those who are not scheduled for one of these ministries can just sit back and passively watch the liturgy around them. This is not correct.

Those who are scheduled to serve a particular mass are first part of the worshipping community; they come forward at a certain moment in time during Mass, serve the community, and then return to their role as part of the worshipping community. We all are part of the ministry of the worshipping community. Liturgy is not a spectator sport!

The baptized are called to participate in song and spoken word, to listen attentively to God's Word, and to exercise their baptismal priesthood in prayer for the Church, the world, and all in need during the Universal Prayer (General Intercessions). Our sincere effort to participate in song, verbal responses, posture, and attitude can encourage others to also respond in kind.

In the celebration of the Mass, the faithful form a holy people, a people whom God has called his own, a royal priesthood, so that they can give thanks to God and offer the spotless Victim not only through the hands of the priest but also together with him, and so that they may learn to offer themselves (GIRM, 95). This is the basis for the "full, conscious, and active participation" of the faithful that is called for by the very nature of liturgy.

LITURGY AND DEVOTIONS

Liturgy is the official, public prayer of the church. Liturgy is something that is done by Jesus Christ; he is present in the Church, especially in her celebrations of the liturgy. The word *liturgy* comes from a Greek term meaning public work. Every liturgical celebration is an action of Christ the High Priest and of his Mystical Body, which is the Church. It therefore requires the participation of the people of God in the work of God.

Whenever we gather for a liturgical celebration, we celebrate Christ's passion, death, resurrection, and glorious ascension and our participation in it. This is so important that we need a whole liturgical year to explore this in all its facets. The Constitution on the Sacred Liturgy (CSL) of Vatican II teaches us that "The liturgy is the summit toward which the activity of the church is directed and the fount from which all her power flows" (CSL, #10).

Liturgy takes many forms; it is more than just the celebration of Eucharist. Some of the more common forms of liturgy include the celebration of the other six sacraments, the Liturgy of the Hours, the Rites of Christian Burial, the Rite of Christian Initiation of Adults (RCIA), and Exposition of the Blessed Sacrament. Each of these liturgies has a unique liturgical book containing the rites and liturgical rubrics associated with it.

Vatican II teaches that our spiritual life is not limited solely to participation in the liturgy, this is where popular devotional practices play a role in helping to foster our prayer. Throughout history, there has been a variety of popular devotional practices. Devotions are external practices that are attached to particular titles for Jesus or Mary, saints, times, pilgrimage sites, places, insignia, medals, or customs (Directory on Popular Piety and the Liturgy, 2001). These private prayers are not meant to replace the liturgical life of the Church, but rather to continue and extend it into daily life. They should be so fashioned that they harmonize with the liturgical season, accord with the sacred liturgy, are in some way derived from it and lead the people to it, since, in fact, the liturgy by its very nature far surpasses any of them (CSL, # 13).

Some examples include the rosary, the Stations of the Cross, and the Angelus. Unlike the seven sacraments, popular devotions cannot be traced directly back to the ministry of Jesus. Most devotions developed gradually as the faithful sought ways of living out their faith. Before Vatican II, the Mass was celebrated in Latin, Communion was infrequent, and church architecture kept people far away from the altar. The faithful would go to church and then pray devotion since they could not understand what was being said.

Vatican II restored the liturgy to the ideals of the early Fathers and removed many popular exercises from the liturgy. The bishops also restored the emphasis on the Word, the sacraments, the Paschal Mystery of Christ. They also recognized the validity of popular devotions, but subordinated them to the liturgy. Since the liturgy is the center of the life of the church, popular devotions should be in harmony with the liturgy, drawing inspiration from it and ultimately leading back to it. Devotions should harmonize with the liturgical season, that's why we pray the Stations of the Cross during Lent. Praying the mysteries of the rosary help us to meditate of Christ's life, death, and resurrection throughout the entire liturgical year. Exposition and adoration of the Blessed Sacrament also help our spiritual life.

Exposition of the Blessed Sacrament either in a monstrance or ciborium is part of liturgy, so there are liturgical norms and Canon laws to be followed. During exposition (meaning the tabernacle doors are open) the praying of devotional prayers such as the rosary or Stations of the Cross are considered devotions and not liturgy so they are not in keeping with the church's teaching of exposition.

During exposition of the Blessed Sacrament it is appropriate to pray the Liturgy of the Hours, read Sacred Scripture, meditate and reflect on Scripture, and just be in the presence of the Lord without doing anything except "waiting on the Lord" to speak to you.

You could have a diary to write down any words the Lord shares with you during this time. Exposition is really about just sitting in the presence of God. Think of exposition of the Blessed Sacrament similar to Mass. Once the host and wine are changed into the Body and Blood of Christ, we don't start praying a rosary or say chaplet prayers. Instead we "adore Christ" by looking upon him when the priest shows the host and the chalice to us.

During adoration of the Blessed Sacrament (meaning the tabernacle doors are closed) private devotional prayers are totally in keeping with the church's teaching of adoration.

Liturgical services are celebrations of the Church, not private functions, meaning they are always communal. Devotions can be performed alone or in a group. Liturgy is the official prayer of the Church, while devotions are prayers whose texts are not contained in the official liturgical books. Liturgy is the center of the life of the Church. Popular devotions are never a substitute for the liturgy, yet they do play a crucial role in helping to foster our prayer life.

Liturgy and Social Justice

The Catholic Church has a rich history of Catholic social teaching that provides certain themes to help us understand what is meant by "justice." The United States Conference of Catholic Bishops (USCCB) has compiled seven themes of Catholic Social Teaching. These themes are Life and Dignity of the Human Person; Call to Family, Community, and Participation; Rights and Responsibilities; Option for the Poor and Vulnerable; The Dignity of Work and the Rights of Workers; Solidarity; and Care for God's Creation. *T*hese mentioning of these themes is only a starting point. A better understanding can be achieved by reading the papal, conciliar, and episcopal documents that make up this rich tradition. One resource is from the USCCB called *"Sharing Catholic Social Teaching: Challenges and Directions."*

Scripture calls us to be faithful to God and to each other. This faithfulness is more than just a call to love God. Faithfulness is a concern for our neighbor and our world. This is what it means to live life with a "justice lens." Our entire Eucharistic liturgy announces this message. Our celebration of the Eucharist is all about social justice. From the moment we share new life in Christ through our baptism, the liturgy requires that we become what we celebrate.

There are many justice moments in our Eucharistic celebration. The theme of justice begins at the liturgy's outset. The Gathering Rite brings all the people of God together as the body of Christ. This gathering is the justice of inclusiveness. It is here that we accept all people as they are in the name of Christ. The Penitential Act invites us to acknowledge our sinfulness, both individually and corporately.

Here we experience the Lord's compassion and mercy as we become bearers of the same mercy to one another.

Throughout the Liturgy of the Word we are constantly reminded of God's justice to all people. Throughout the entire liturgical year, the theme of justice permeates the Word. It is this ever present justice that we carry into the Liturgy of the Eucharist. Whether we are contemplating the preparation of the altar and gifts or the wholeness of salvation history that is presented during the Eucharistic Prayer, the notion of God's justice is ever present throughout.

The Eucharistic Prayers speak of God's justice throughout salvation history. The second Eucharistic Prayer for Reconciliation, for example, reminds us of what God has done for us through Jesus. The preface of this prayer has powerful justice phrase: "For though the human race is divided by dissension and discord, yet we know that by testing us you change our hearts to prepare them for reconciliation" (EP Reconciliation II).

During the Communion Rite, we receive the Body and Blood of Christ. The Church teaches that we are to be the justice of God and become the body of Christ to the world. In the Dismissal Rite, we receive a commission: "Go in peace glorifying the Lord by your life." These words send us forth to carry out the will and justice of God. Pope John Paul II in his apostolic letter Mane Nobiscum Domine (Stay with Us, Lord) preached, "Authentic celebration and adoration of the Eucharist that does not lead to mission does not exist."

After exploring the Catholic Bishops' seven key themes concerning our Catholic teaching and the way this justice is proclaimed throughout our liturgies, we now will briefly examine how the Scriptures in each liturgical season handle justice.

At the beginning of the liturgical year, Scripture presents a vision of the reign of God. Advent emphasizes in particular the themes of protecting the poor and venerable as well as living in solidarity. During the Christmas season, we find examples of texts that express or connect to the bishops' second theme: family, community, and participation. Here we listen to story after story of unexpected heroes Mary, Joseph, Zachariah, the shepherds, and the magi. All had their reasons for being excluded, but were welcomed by God.

During Lent, the Scriptures highlight the theme relating to the dignity of every human being. The stories from John's gospel used for the scrutinies remind us that each life is valuable and valued. A consistent theme of Catholic social teaching reflected in the celebration of Triduum is that the poor and vulnerable person rejected by the community is the very person through whom we are healed and brought to new life. During the Easter season, the Acts of the Apostles proclaim the theme of rights and responsibilities, as the disciples attempted to create a just society.

The Lectionary during ordinary time describes what the first disciples were called to do and be. These Gospels tell us, that to be a disciple of Christ is to serve those who are poor and vulnerable. The theme of respecting the dignity of work and the rights of workers is evident in the way Jesus uses images of labor and workers in his teachings. In the psalms we sing about the justice theme of care for all of God's creation.

The Scriptures that are proclaimed throughout the liturgical year teach us the link between liturgy and justice. St. Pope John Paul II in his homily on the year of the Eucharist taught, "Eucharist and mission are two inseparable realities." Liturgy models the justice of God; our lives should do the same.

O ANTIPHONS

Advent announces the season which anticipates the coming of Christ at Christmas. The last eight days of Advent form a little season all by themselves. As the church prepares for the feast of Christmas, the liturgy gets more intense. At daily Mass, the Gospels relate the events leading up to the first Christmas. At evening prayer, we have a special series of antiphons which beckon the Messiah to come. Each night gives him a new name, drawn from the Old Testament. These names are "O Wisdom," "O Sacred Lord," "O Flower of Jesse's Stem," "O Key of David," "O Radiant Dawn," "O King of All Nations," and the greatest of them all, "O Emmanuel," a name that means "God is with us."

For obvious reasons, the church calls these refrains the "O Antiphons," a hallmark of Advent. By the middle ages, those seven antiphons got strung together into a popular hymn. The last one became verse one and "O Come, O Come, Emmanuel" was born. Thus, the antiphon originally established for the last evening before Christmas Eve is now often sung during the Advent season itself.

The "O Antiphons" are so called because each addresses the Coming One with a messianic title from the Hebrew Scriptures, preceded by the exclamation "O." These biblical refrains are tied to the Magnificat because this was Mary's response to the news of the Messiah's impending birth and because she is the pre-eminent Advent person, who knew so well how to wait for the Lord and then how to act when invited to do so.

The structure of each antiphon is the same for the entire week. One or more titles, predicating certain attributes to the Messiah, followed by a petition to come and accomplish in the hearts and lives of believers what needs to be done to establish the Messiah's kingdom in all its fullness. All the antiphons are biblical, filled with imagery from the Torah, the prophets, and the Wisdom literature. These prayers provide the church with a late-Advent refresher course on the identity of the One whom we expect.

According to Professor Robert Greenberg of the San Francisco Conservatory of Music, the Benedictine monks arranged these antiphons with a definite purpose. If one starts with the last title and takes the first letter of each one—*E*mmanuel, *R*ex, *O*riens, *C*lavis, *R*adix, *A*donai, *S*apientia—the Latin words *ero cras* are formed, meaning, "Tomorrow, I will come."

Therefore, the Lord Jesus, whose coming we have prepared for in Advent and whom we have addressed in these seven Messianic titles, now speaks to us, "Tomorrow, I will come." So the "O" Antiphons not only bring intensity to our Advent preparation, but bring it to a joyful conclusion.

In reviewing these antiphons, it is important to remember the various titles are not primarily geared to an Advent observance which looks longingly and sentimentally to the coming of the helpless Babe of Bethlehem. Rather in accordance with the liturgical thrust of Advent, the titles are those traditionally associated with the Messiah, King, and Lord. As the late Scripture scholar, Fr. Raymond Brown, has stressed in his reflection on the infancy narratives, the church directs our thoughts to receive "an adult Christ at Christmas."

During Advent we hear these "O" Antiphons in our readings, and they are part of our sung prayer. They are part of the prayer of the church. Let us continue this Advent to wait in hope and joy as we prepare for the coming of our Savior, Christ the King.

O Come, O Come, Emmanuel!

EXPOSITION VS. ADORATION

Questions and Answers

Q1: Did I do something wrong by praying the rosary during my hour of adoration?

A: Absolutely not! Praying quietly before the Blessed Sacrament is a time honored tradition in the church. And we believe that the mysteries of the holy rosary lead people to Christ, which makes this very appropriate.

The concern is in the "verbal praying" among groups, which tends to break the silence of a chapel where it is best to avoid such things out of respect for others. Most parishes have ample spaces to gather for group prayer.

During the Rite of Exposition when specific prayers are being said aloud and songs are being sung, it would not be appropriate to be praying a rosary, just as it is not appropriate to pray a rosary during the liturgy of the Mass.

As will be explained in a later answer (Q10), praying any devotional prayer in front of the exposed Eucharist should be done silently and reverently. Praying devotional prayers out loud might disturb someone else who comes to adore the Blessed Sacrament in the quiet of their heart.

Q2: Why do we have Eucharistic Exposition and adoration? A: There are many reasons to spend time with the Lord in Eucharistic Exposition (meaning, you see Jesus either in the monstrance or ciborium, when the tabernacle doors are open) or in adoration (when the tabernacle doors are closed and Jesus sees you). Some of them include an opportunity to draw us more deeply into the mystery of Christ's real presence in the Holy Eucharist, to strengthen our relationship with Jesus Christ, and to express our love, gratitude, and respect for Christ our Lord.

Q3: What's the difference between Eucharistic Exposition and adoration according to the Church?

A: Exposition of the Blessed Sacrament, when the door of the tabernacle is open so that Blessed Sacrament is visible, is part of liturgy, so there are liturgical norms and Canon laws to be followed. Adoration of the Blessed Sacrament, when the door of the tabernacle is closed, is a private devotion.

Q4: What does the church mean by liturgy?

A: Liturgy is the official, public prayer of the Church. Liturgy is something that is done by Jesus Christ; he is present in the church. The word *liturgy* comes from a Greek term meaning work of the people.

The Constitution on the Sacred Liturgy #26 teaches us that "Liturgical services are not private functions, but are celebrations of the Church." In other words, if there is a liturgical ritual book approved by the Holy Father, required for any given liturgical rite, then it is considered liturgy. Within the liturgical ritual book, there are guidelines for Exposition of the Blessed Sacrament. More explanation about prayer in the presence of the Blessed Sacrament during Exposition is given in a later answer (Q10).

Q5: What are some other examples of liturgy other than Exposition of the Blessed Sacrament?

A: Some of the more common forms of liturgy include the celebration of the other six sacraments, the Liturgy of the Hours, the Order of Christian Funerals, and the Rite of Christian Initiation of Adults (RCIA). Each of these liturgies has a unique liturgical book containing the rites and liturgical rubrics associated with it.

Q6: What are some examples of popular devotions?

A: There are many devotions approved by the Catholic Church; some of the more common ones include the rosary, the Stations of the Cross, the Angelus, and the making of a pilgrimage.

Q7: How do popular devotions fit into our liturgical life?

A: The Second Vatican Council teaches that our spiritual life is not limited solely to participation in the liturgy; this is where popular devotional practices play a role in helping to foster our prayer. Throughout history, there has been a variety of popular devotional practices. Devotions are external practices that are attached to particular titles for Jesus or Mary, saints, times, pilgrimage sites, places, insignia, medals, or customs.

Q8: Do we also adore Christ during Mass?

A: Exposition of the Blessed Sacrament is similar to the showing of the Body and of the Blood of Christ after the consecration at Mass. Once the host and wine are changed into the Body and Blood of Christ, we do adore Christ by looking upon him when the priest lifts the host, the Body of Christ, and the chalice containing the Blood of Christ for us to see. During this part of the Mass we totally focus on Our Lord, without saying other devotional prayers such as the rosary, Stations of the Cross, or chaplet prayers. Praying these devotions is not appropriate when we should be participating fully in the liturgy of the Mass.

Q9: When did the distinction happen between liturgy and devotion?

A: Since the Second Vatican Council, Eucharistic Exposition and benediction are no longer considered devotions, but rather are a part of the Church's official liturgy. Whereas in the past benediction was frequently added on to the end of another service or devotion, this is no longer permitted. Eucharistic Exposition and benediction are each complete liturgical services in their own right and are to be celebrated as such.

Q10: How does this distinction of liturgy and devotion affect how we pray in the Blessed Sacrament Chapel?

A: One of the main tenets to remember is that there should be a respectful silence in the Blessed Sacrament chapel so all who enter may pray, reflect, and just be in the presence of the Lord without being interrupted by another person or group praying a devotional prayer out loud.

The personal praying and reflecting on a decade of the rosary in silence, for example, would not disturb someone who has come to adore the Lord, since only God would hear your prayer. On the other hand, praying that same rosary out loud could interfere with someone's need for their quiet, focused time with Jesus.

During exposition (meaning the tabernacle doors are open) the praying of devotional prayers out loud such as the Stations of the Cross or the rosary is not in keeping with the Church's understanding of Exposition of the Blessed Sacrament.

Q11: If I want to say a rosary out loud with a group of friends or family members, how should I do it?

A: In order to keep the respectful silence in the Blessed Sacrament Chapel, you could move to sacred space for praying the rosary, and then return to the Blessed Sacrament Chapel for your time with the Lord in Eucharistic Exposition.

Red, White, and Blue Masses

Contrary to what some might think, a Liturgy of the Eucharist, which has been termed a Red, White, or Blue Mass is not a Mass we celebrate on the Fourth of July. The designation of a Red, White, or Blue Mass also does not necessarily imply the color of the vestment a priest will wear during the celebration, since blue is not a liturgical color. It certainly is not a Mass we pray as a community in hopes that God will bless your favorite sports team with a win. Actually, there are Masses in the Roman Missal for particular groups, for certain liturgical days, or for certain sacramental or other occasions that often are referred to by special names, and Red, White, and Blue Masses fall into this category.

The traditional Red Mass is an annual event in most dioceses and archdioceses and asks the Holy Spirit to guide all those who seek justice. It is a special Mass for judges, attorneys, law professors, and their students, as well as government officials in the legislative and executive branches. The yearly Red Mass in Washington marks the opening of the judicial year for the U.S. Supreme Court and is usually attended by several Supreme Court justices and many other high government officials. Dating from the Middle Ages, the Red Mass gets its name from the English tradition of red as the academic robe or hood color for those with law degrees. A red vestment would be worn by the celebrant.

More recently, in the United States dioceses, since September 11, 2001, many parishes hold a yearly Blue Mass for police, firefighters, first responders, and others in law enforcement. The Blue Mass dates back to 1934, when a Catholic priest from the Archdiocese of Baltimore, Maryland, organized the Catholic Police and Firemen's

Society while stationed at St. Patrick Church in Washington DC. More than 1,000 police and firemen, dressed in their blue uniforms, attended that first Blue Mass. The tradition of showing gratitude to emergency responders and their families in this way has continued throughout the United States.

Parishes who celebrate a yearly White Mass remember doctors, nurses, and all in the health care profession. The annual White Mass recognizes the ministry of those who protect life and care for the ill and dying. These healthcare professionals are really ambassadors of mercy, showing their compassion to all in medical need. Throughout the church year, the color white liturgically is prescribed as the vestment color during Easter time and Christmas time; on the Solemnity of the Most Holy Trinity; and on other celebrations of the Lord and the Blessed Virgin Mary. When a White Mass is celebrated, white vestments are often worn, reflecting the white coat most commonly worn by those in the medical field. Red, White, and Blue Masses get their names not from the Mass vestments, but from the traditional colors worn by the groups we are remembering, praying for, and for whom we are demonstrating appreciation.

The *General Instruction of the Roman Missal* (GIRM) has a section entitled "Masses and Prayers for Various Needs and Occasions." In this section of the Roman Missal, Holy Mother Church provides us many opportunities to celebrate liturgies that may be used in the various occasions of Christian life for the needs of the whole world or for the needs of the Church, whether universal or local (GIRM, #368). During a Red, White, or Blue Mass, we would use this section of the Roman Missal for the prayers our celebrant would pray. There are many options that may be prayed for each celebration. Once example of the Collect (the Opening Prayer) that could be used for a Blue Mass is the following: "O God, who arrange all things in wondrous order and govern in marvelous ways, look with favor on the assembled, for whom we now pray, and mercifully pour out upon them the spirit of your wisdom, that they may decide everything for the well-being and peace of all and may never turn aside from your will. Through our Lord Jesus Christ, your Son, who lives and reigns with you in the unity of the Holy Spirit, one God, for ever and ever" (Roman Missal, For Civil Needs, # 23, For a Governing Assembly).

Throughout the liturgical year, there are a variety of prayers we can use depending on the needs of the local or universal church such as prayers speaking about civil disturbance, the preservation of peace and justice, and for the sanctification of human labor. We are very fortunate to celebrate liturgies such as Red, White, and Blue Masses, since they help all of us to truly live the Paschal Mystery of Jesus through our daily lives.

Sacred Silence

In the celebration of Mass, we are called to raise our hearts and minds to God. We do this in a variety of ways with the postures of standing, kneeling, and sitting, through our sung and spoken prayer, and also by our silent reflection. This sacred silence is part of what the Constitution on the Sacred Liturgy calls part of our full, conscious, and active participation (*CSL,* #14). These times of sacred silence during the Mass are not merely times when nothing happens; rather, they are opportunities for us to enter more deeply into what God is doing in the celebration of the Eucharist.

The Bishops of the United States remind us, "Holy Mother church has prepared for us throughout our Eucharist this sacred silence to help us spend time with the Lord individually and as a community. Silence in the Liturgy allows the community to reflect on what it has heard and experienced and to open its heart to the mystery celebrated" (Sing to the Lord, Music in Divine Worship, #118).

We are invited to silence several times during the Mass. We gather in silence before Mass begins so that each of us can leave the concerns of the outside world and prepare ourselves to enter into the sacred action. We are then called to silence during the Penitential Act as we recall and repent of our sins. We have brief periods of silence after each reading to reflect on the words of sacred scripture. After the homily we spend time in silence to allow the Holy Spirit to help us personally understand the words of the homilist in a way that make us better people. The *General Instruction of the Roman Missal* (GIRM) teaches through "brief periods of silence…under the action of the Holy Spirit, the Word of God may be grasped by the heart and a response through prayer may be prepared" (*GIRM,* #56). We take time for silent reflection and prayer after Holy Communion as we ask the Lord to fill us with his love and to give him thanks for the great blessings he has given us.

Sacred silence at Mass allows us to ponder all the beauty and benefits the Most Holy Sacrifice of the Mass has to offer. These periods of silence are intended to bring reality into focus. Pope emeritus Benedict XVI once described sacred silence as "a positive stillness." He meant that our silence in prayer is not to be a meditation alone. Instead, silence during our prayer celebration is an occasion to more deeply understand the Mass itself. Sacred silence in the liturgy punctuates a rich and profound time of prayer with opportunities to reflect on the reality of our liturgical experience. Silence isn't easy for any of us. The church gives us this sacred silence to hear the voice of the Lord. May we all grow in our love of sacred silence!

The Stations of the Cross

The devotional prayer form that is most often associated with the holy season of Lent is the Stations of the Cross. Throughout this devotion, the faithful offer a living witness to the Passion and death of Jesus. This prayer has its foundation from the ancient practice of going on a pilgrimage to the Holy Land. The last section of the pilgrimage was to walk on the Via Dolorosa, or Way of Sadness. The Via Dolorosa is the route that Jesus presumably took through Jerusalem to Calvary with his cross. The stations are actually based on Sacred Scripture, each station is where Jesus stopped along the road.

Over the centuries, the number of stations has varied from just a few to over thirty. The Stations of the Cross became standardized back in the sixteenth century, giving us the last of his fourteen stops. Some versions of the Stations of the Cross consist of a fifteen station; which would be the remembrance of his Resurrection. Originally, the stations were associated with the Franciscan order, since they were responsible to protect the Holy Land.

The history of the Stations of the Cross goes back to when Emperor Constantine permitted Christians to legally worship in the Roman Empire in the year 313. Before that, Christians were persecuted for their faith. By 335, Constantine erected the Church of the Holy Sepulcher. This is on the location where Christians believe Jesus was placed in the tomb on Good Friday. Once the building was completed, many pilgrims especially during Holy Week started taking pilgrimages.

A French pilgrim named Egeria documented in her diary the beginnings of these pilgrimages which took place in the fourth century. She states the pilgrims began at the place where Jesus's Agony in the Garden happened on Holy Thursday night and then eventually the pilgrims continued to Jerusalem. She explains the pilgrimages eventually took a fixed route from where Pilate had his judgment hall, to the Church of the Holy Sepulcher. That route through Jerusalem continues today. It is now known as the Via Dolorosa, Latin for the "Sorrowful Way."

Egeria noted that stops developed on the way to show specific events on the road to Calvary. In some spots, those on the pilgrimage could only guess where some incidents took place because Jerusalem had been almost completely destroyed by Roman armies in AD 70.

It took some time for the depictions described in the stations to become commonplace in churches. Pope Innocent XI permitted the Franciscans to actually display these stations in all the churches where the Franciscans were living. While we expect to see the Stations of the Cross in every church we visit, originally they were always outside and not part of a church building. Pope Benedict XIII offered indulgences to all the faithful whenever they visited these holy sites. This continues today provided faithful follow the usual requirements. Pope Clement XII allowed all churches to have stations inside the church building and fixed the number at fourteen. Today some churches have included the Resurrection as a fifteenth station. The Stations of the Cross are not required, yet these beloved images are found in almost every church.

The Bishop's document on Liturgical Environment states, "Whether celebrated by a community or by individuals, the Stations of the Cross offer a way for the faithful to enter more fully into the passion and death of the Lord and to serve as another manifestation of the pilgrim Church on its homeward journey. Traditionally the stations have been arranged around the walls of the nave of the church, or, in some instances, around the gathering space or even the exterior of the church, marking the devotion as a true journey" (*Built of Living Stones, Art, Architecture and Worship,* #133). Pictures or tableaux of the various stations are not necessary, since it is the actual cross associated with each station that is our focal point.

There are numerous versions of the Stations of the Cross available with each one having a different perspective. Pope Saint John Paul II wrote a Scriptural Way of the Cross. This version is closely aligned with Sacred Scripture. His version contains the following fourteen stations: Jesus in the garden of Gethsemane; Jesus is betrayed by Judas and arrested; Jesus is condemned by the Sanhedrin; Jesus is denied by Peter; Jesus is judged by Pilate; Jesus is scourged and crowned with thorns; Jesus takes up his cross; Simon helps Jesus carry his cross; Jesus meets the daughters of Jerusalem; Jesus is crucified; Jesus promises a place in his kingdom to the good thief; Jesus entrusts Mary and John to each other; Jesus dies on the cross; Jesus is laid in the tomb.

While the liturgy is the summit toward which the activity of the Church is directed and the font from which all her power flows, popular devotional practices such as the Stations of the Cross play a crucial role in helping to foster our ceaseless prayer.

UNDERSTANDING LITURGY
LITURGICAL BOOKS (HISTORY AND QUALITY)

In the first several centuries, the texts used for liturgy were written on a papyrus scroll with a spindle on each end. That is the same style of liturgical book used in the time of Jesus. We read in Luke 4:18–20 how Jesus went to the temple and was asked to minister as the reader. St. Luke tells us "He [Jesus] picked up a scroll, proclaimed the reading and then handed the scroll back to the attendant." You can see this type of liturgical book still used in a synagogue.

As Christianity spreads, the use of papyrus develops into the use of folded animal skin gathered into a book for the writing of liturgical texts. This new format was much more durable. They were copied by hand and allowed a reader access to individual pages rather than needing to unroll a very long scroll.

The next phase occurred around the time of the invention of the printing press. This mechanical printing coincided with all the prayer texts and the lectionary being standardized for all Roman Rite churches. One of the main reasons for the standardized texts was to eliminate the local variations that were occurring and to bring under the same umbrella conformity to a universal model.

The collection of texts into books allowed the Church to organize these collections into categories. These included Missals or Sacramentaries which contained the prayers and readings used for Mass, books used by the Bishop called Pontificals, Breviaries containing the Liturgy of the Hours and all the other ritual books needed to celebrate other rites.

The computer has had a tremendous effect on the process we use to compose liturgical books. Our current technology guarantees all liturgical books published will have the exact wording in each prayer no matter who is the actual publisher.

The digital files for the publication of the third edition of the Roman Missal, that's the missal we are using currently, were given to seven different publishers. Each created a beautiful Missal with the exact wording and punctuation. They were able to customize their publication of the Missal through the use of placing special pictures throughout each book, choosing the font settings, the specialized paper quality, and other such print medium options.

Throughout each successive format all of the official liturgical books were always treated with respect. We reverence them as signs and symbols of sacred realities. We experience this particularly in the Book of the Gospel as we carry it in procession, surround it with candles, incense it and kiss it. All of our liturgical books remind us of our great tradition in salvation history.

In every liturgy we use a variety of images, music, lights, flowers, and choreography. You also find items from creation such as wine, water, bread, fire, and oil. These help to engage our senses as we offer our praise and thanks to God. The books used in our liturgical celebrations must also be visually attractive and impressive-looking. We do not use flimsy pamphlets which depict a disposable or trivial piece of information contained in those volumes. The Lectionary for Mass (LM) states, "Since in liturgical celebrations the books serve as signs and symbols of the higher realities, care must be taken to ensure they are truly worthy, dignified and beautiful" (LM, # 35). These liturgical books help our community find holiness in the sacramental interaction with material elements.

The books we use throughout our liturgies are initially approved by the Vatican for the universal Church. The next step involves the bishops' conference of each language grouping (i.e., English, Spanish, and Italian, etc.). The bishops work together on their individual translation and adaptation. In the English version, many of the texts are translated by ICEL (The International Commission on English in the Liturgy). Scripture references are always taken from one of the approved translations. All of the texts used in each translation must be approved by the bishops' conference and then confirmed by the Vatican before they are actually published. This process usually takes years from start to finish.

We use a variety of books throughout our liturgical celebrations, depending on the rite to be celebrated. Most often we use the Roman Missal, which contains the prayers used for the celebration of Mass and the Lectionary for Mass, which contains the readings proclaimed during Mass. The Book of the Gospel contains only the Gospel readings for Mass. It is used mostly for Sunday celebrations, holy days, and special feast days. Another liturgical book, containing four volumes, is the *Liturgy of the Hours*. It is also known as the Divine Office and is the daily prayer of the church, marking the hours of each day and sanctifying the day with prayer. All the clergy and many lay people pray the Hours every day.

There are many other liturgical books approved by the Vatican. The following are the ones normally used throughout the liturgical year; most relate to the celebration of the sacraments and include: *Rite of Baptism*, *Rite of Penance*, *Rite of Christian Initiation of Adults*, *Pastoral Care of the Sick*, *Rite of Marriage*, *Holy Communion and Worship of the Eucharist Outside of Mass*, *Order of Christian Funerals*, and *Book of Blessings*.

In the liturgy, gestures are always accompanied by words. The beauty of the liturgy is first and foremost the beauty of Christ. The liturgical books we use help us to celebrate, pray, and live the mystery of Christ in the dignity and the beauty of its celebration. These liturgical books deserve to be worthy instruments of our celebration.

THE SIGN OF PEACE

The custom of Christians kissing goes clear back to the New Testament. St. Paul urged Christians to greet one another with a holy kiss (Romans 16:16). The priest kisses the altar both during the gathering song and then again during the closing song. The deacon, priest, or bishop kisses the Gospel book after the Gospel is proclaimed. We are asked to offer each other a sign (kiss) of peace.

Kissing the altar first appeared in the fourth century. People used to kiss the threshold of the building they entered in respect. At Mass the kiss switched to the altar, which symbolized Christ and the holy place where Mass will follow. Kissing the Gospel book follows the same thought. We recognize the presence of Christ in the book that speaks good news. The kiss of the altar at the end of the Mass is the farewell counterpart of the entrance kiss.

The sign of peace is a ritual that was part of the early church. In the ancient Middle East, where we get the roots of Christianity, the members of the church actually kissed each other instead of just shaking hands. Vatican II recovered this ancient ritual of reconciliation and unity. The placement of the sign of peace has varied over the centuries from after the intercessions, to before communion. For a while it was not even a part of the church ritual. Since the Second Vatican Council, the exchange of peace comes after the consecration because it refers to, as Pope Francis states, "the 'paschal kiss' of the risen Christ present on the altar." It comes just before the breaking of the bread during which "the Lamb of God is implored to give us his peace."

This is not the same as a greeting before Mass. While the actions may look similar, they are very different. There is a difference between the greetings that we offer one another before Mass begins and the actual sign of peace exchanged before the Communion rite. The greeting of parishioners before Mass is just that, a greeting. Before Mass we take the time to find out who is part of our worshipping community, to know their names and recognize them as members of the Body of Christ. It is not part of the church's ritual. On the other hand, the sign of peace before Communion helps us to reconcile our lives with those around us. It helps us to build unity among the people of God. This action is a prayer. Different cultures express this prayer of reconciliation and unity in a variety of ways (i.e., a kiss, an embrace, a bow, or a handshake).

The words of the *General Instruction of the Roman Missal* (GIRM) regarding the Rite of Peace state, "The Church entreats peace and unity for herself and for the whole human family, and the faithful express to each other their ecclesial communion and mutual charity before communicating in the Sacrament" (GIRM, # 82). This teaching reminds us to take this liturgical act seriously. It must be done with dignity and awareness. We should remember it is not a liturgical form of "good morning," but a witness to the Christian belief that true peace is a gift of Christ's death and resurrection. When a priest or deacon at mass invites us to "offer each other a sign of peace" it is a reminder that Christ is our divine peace.

The Universal Prayer

During the liturgy of the Word we listen, sing, and reflect on Sacred Scripture. Following the homily and the Profession of Faith we then pray The Universal Prayer or what is also known as the Prayer of the Faithful or General Intercessions. Since Vatican II we have prayed the Universal Prayer at every Mass. In different parts of the world this prayer is also called the Prayer of the Faithful or Bidding Prayer. Many of you may remember also calling it the General Intercessions.

This prayer is universal since the assembly prays for all the needs of the world, not just for any local needs. This prayer is also the "Prayer of the Faithful" since the catechumens are dismissed from Mass before we start praying this prayer, so the faithful (those who are baptized) are exercising their priestly ministry (*General Instruction of the Roman Missal*, # 69). They could also be called a bidding prayer since these prayers are composed as a litany and someone is mentioning each part of the intention and bids the rest of the assembly to respond in prayer.

In the Universal Prayer, the gathered assembly responds in faith and hope to the Word of God by petitioning God on behalf of the whole world. The prayer is composed of three parts: an introduction by the priest, the petition with a response by the people, and a conclusion by the priest. The church gives us the structure of these intentions as follows: for the needs of the church; for public authorities and the salvation of the whole world; for those burdened by any kind of difficulty; and for the local community (*General Instruction of the Roman Missal*, # 70).

The Universal Prayer intentions are intercessions, not announcements, prayers of thanksgiving, or prayers of praise. They are not directed to the Blessed Virgin Mary or to any particular saint. The adding of any devotional prayer, even to the Blessed Mother, is not prescribed by the General Instruction, since holy Mother Church teaches, "These intentions are offered to God for the salvation of all" (Roman Missal, #69).

It would not be appropriate to make these prayers specific or personal because liturgy is communal, not private. Petitions inviting the assembly to "add their own intercessions in silence" are not in the spirit of the "Universal" Prayer. We gather as the body of Christ. This means the priest, deacon, and the rest of the worshipping community are exercising their roles by praying on behalf of all the people of the Church and even the whole world.

The Universal Prayer is part of the liturgy of the Word, so it is crafted from the Sacred Scripture proclaimed from each daily or Sunday Mass. Those who pray the Liturgy of the Hours, "Morning Prayer," and "Evening Prayer" will find similar intercessions as part of the structure of "Lauds" and "Vespers." Intercessions also occur in the Eucharistic Prayer, which occurs after the Sanctus (Holy, Holy, Holy).

Today the Universal Prayer is integral to every celebration of the Mass. When a deacon is present, it is part of his ministry to announce these petitions. This tradition goes back to the practice from the fourth century *Apostolic Constitution,* since the deacon is the person responsible for charity in the community. The deacon's ministry makes him very aware of the needs of the local community, so it makes sense for him to lead us in praying for these needs.

A more formal expression of the General Intercessions occurs on Good Friday. On this day, the celebrant, deacon, or other minister intones solemn intercessory prayers that are followed by silent prayer and are then concluded with another prayer intoned by the priest followed by the assembly's "Amen." During this celebration of the Triduum, there are ten intentions proclaimed and include petitions for the Holy Church, the pope, for the faithful, for catechumens, for the unity of Christians, for the Jewish people, for those who do not believe in Christ, for those who do not believe in God, for those in public office, and for those in tribulation.

Pope Saint John Paul II wrote, "The Universal Prayer responds not only to the needs of a particular Christian community but also to those of all humanity" (*Deis Domini-On Keeping the Lord's Day Holy*, # 38). When we pray the Universal Prayer, we join the rest of the universal church as we pray for all the needs of people throughout the world.

The Mass

The celebration of Mass, as the action of Christ and the People of God arrayed hierarchically, is the center of the whole Christian life for the Church both universal and local, as well as for each of the faithful individually. (*General Instruction of the Roman Missal: Chapter 1, no. 16*)

THE INTRODUCTORY RITES OF THE MASS

Mass consists of two main sections: the Liturgy of the Word and the Liturgy of the Eucharist. The rites that precede the liturgy of the Word are called the Introductory Rites. The purpose of the Introductory Rites according to the *General Instruction of the Roman Missal* (GIRM) is "that the faithful who come together as one establish communion and dispose themselves to listen properly to God's word and to celebrate Eucharist worthily" (GIRM, #46*)*. This means all that comes before the Liturgy of the Word is intended to help us gather as a community and prepare to celebrate the Sacred Mysteries.

The Mass begins "when the people have gathered" or "Populo congregato" in Latin with the Entrance Song. The current Roman Missal is very clear about the importance of the active participation of the people. Before Vatican II, the rubric in Latin was "Sacerdos paratus" meaning "When the priest is ready." This shows the responsibility we have concerning our purpose. Eucharist is the source and summit of our lives, so we gather to praise and thank God while receiving the sustenance needed to be the Lord's disciple.

Singing has always enlivened Christian worship. The Last Supper ended with a hymn, Paul and Silas sang hymns, the 150 Psalms of David have been sung as early as the sixth century, and Pope Gregory the Great composed music for Entrance Antiphons and Introits.

During our liturgical tradition certain Introits were eventually assigned to specific liturgical days. Each Sunday started to become known by the first word of the Introit. We still carry this tradition today. We speak about the third Sunday of Advent as "Guadete Sunday," from the Introit "Rejoice" and Laetare Sunday on the fourth Sunday of Lent. Many church documents from encyclicals to instructions are also known by the opening words or phrases in Latin.

Prior to Vatican II the priest would say the Introit right before he said the Kyrie (Lord, have mercy). Since the reforms of the Second Vatican Council, the Introit has returned to its original purpose, which we now term the Gathering or Entrance Song.

When the entrance procession begins, we stand and join in prayerful song. The purpose of singing at this time "is to open the celebration, foster the unity of those who have been gathered, introduce their thoughts to the mystery of the liturgical season or festivity, and accompany the procession of the priest and ministers" (GIRM, #47).

The celebrant and other ministers then enter in procession and reverence the altar with a bow (laity) and/or a kiss (clergy). The altar is a symbol of Christ at the heart of the assembly and so deserves this special reverence. During this procession, the Book of the Gospel is placed on the altar. Honor has been shown to this book since the fifth century.

All make the sign of the cross and the celebrant extends a greeting to the gathered people in words taken from Scripture. The Penitential Act follows the greeting. At the very beginning of the Mass, we, the faithful, recall our sins and place our trust in God's abiding mercy. The Penitential Act includes the Kyrie Eleison, a Greek phrase meaning, "Lord, have mercy." This litany recalls God's merciful actions throughout history. On Sundays, especially in Easter time, in place of the customary Penitential Act, the blessing and sprinkling of water to recall Baptism may take place.

On Sundays, solemnities, and feasts, the Gloria follows the Penitential Act. The Gloria begins by echoing the proclamation of the angels at the birth of Christ: "Glory to God in the highest!" In this ancient hymn, the gathered assembly joins the heavenly choirs in offering praise and adoration to the Father and Jesus through the Holy Spirit.

The Introductory Rites conclude with an opening prayer, called the Collect. The celebrant invites the gathered assembly to pray and, after a brief silence, proclaims the prayer of the day. The Collect gathers the prayers of all into one and disposes all to hear the Word of God in the context of the celebration.

These Introductory Rites are important because they focus us on our communal prayer in Christ and help prepare us for listening to God's sacred Word. In our next installment we will examine the part of the Mass called the Liturgy of the Word.

THE LITURGY OF THE WORD

One of the greatest contributions of Vatican II was the revision of the *Lectionary for Mass.* Before The Second Vatican Council there was only a one-year cycle of readings in the Lectionary. Catholics only had the opportunity to hear about one percent of the Old Testament, and about twenty percent of the New Testament.

In 1963 the bishops wanted to renew the life of the Church. One way this was accomplished was to have the people of God hear more sacred Scripture at Mass. The revision expanded the Lectionary to a three-year cycle of readings. Now Catholics hear about fifteen percent of the Old Testament and almost seventy-five percent of the New Testament.

In the liturgy of the Word, the Church feeds the people of God from the table of his Word (*Constitution on the Sacred Liturgy, # 51*). The Scriptures are the Word of God, written under the inspiration of the Holy Spirit. In the Scriptures, God speaks to us, leading us along the path to salvation.

The liturgy of the Word is made up of readings from Scripture. On Sundays and solemnities, there are three Scripture readings. During most of the year, the first reading is from the Old Testament and the second reading is from one of the New Testament letters. During Easter Time, the first reading is from the Acts of the Apostles. The last reading is always proclaimed from one of the four Gospels.

The Responsorial Psalm is sung between the readings. The psalm helps us to meditate on the Word of God. The Psalm that follows the First Reading is "responsorial" because of its form, not because of its function. This psalm is designed to be sung in alternation between the psalmist and the assembly, that's the reason why it's called responsorial. The Psalm usually echoes the theme of the first reading. It is sung from the ambo since it comes from Sacred Scripture.

The high point of the Liturgy of the Word is the proclamation of the Gospel. Because the Gospels tell of the life, ministry, and preaching of Christ, it receives several special signs of honor and reverence. The gathered assembly stands to hear the Gospel and it's introduced by an acclamation of praise. Apart from Lent, the Gospel Acclamation is some musical version of "Alleluia," which is derived from a Hebrew phrase meaning "Praise the Lord!"

This Gospel Acclamation announces the coming of the Gospel and accompanies the procession to the ambo; candles and incense may also accompany the procession. The 2002 *General Instruction of the Roman Missal* (GIRM) confirmed a custom that really had a wide practice earlier in the church. The rubric in this latest GIRM, has the assembly sign themselves on the forehead, lips, and breast as the deacon or priest does. In making the triple sign of the cross, the faithful ask God to bless their minds and hearts so they will accept the Gospel message proclaimed by the priest or deacon, and then proclaim it themselves through their lips and through their lives. Following the Gospel Acclamation, the deacon (or, if no deacon is present, a priest) proclaims the Gospel.

After the Scripture readings, the celebrant or deacon preaches the homily. Here, the homilist focuses on the Scripture texts or some other texts from the liturgy, drawing from them lessons that may help us to live better lives, more faithful to Christ's call to grow in holiness.

On Sundays and Solemnities, the Profession of Faith (the Creed) follows the homily, the Creed unifies all the voices of those gathered in the assembly into the *common faith* we profess. When baptismal promises are renewed (e.g. during the Easter Vigil or at a Mass where we celebrate the Sacrament of a Baptism or Confirmation), they take the place of the Creed.

The liturgy of the Word concludes with the Universal Prayer (the Prayer of the Faithful). The gathered assembly intercedes with God on behalf of the church, the world, and themselves, entrusting their needs to the faithful and loving God.

In the hearing of God's Word, the Church is built up and grows. In the Liturgy of the Word, Christians come together to listen to God's Word in Sacred Scripture, which helps us to grow in faith and become more conformed to the mind of Christ.

THE PREPARATION OF THE ALTAR AND GIFTS

The set of ceremonies that precedes the Eucharistic Prayer is called the preparation of the altar and gifts. This is when the corporal, Roman Missal, and the priest's chalice and the purificators are placed on the altar. The gifts of bread and wine are then brought to the altar in procession by members of the faithful and are accompanied by song. The *General Instruction of the Roman Missal* (GIRM) teaches, "It is desirable that the faithful express their participation by making an offering, bringing forward bread and wine for the celebration of the Eucharist and perhaps other gifts to relieve the needs of the Church and the poor" (GIRM, # 22).

The stewardship of treasure collected for the poor, the community, and for the sacramental table is an important ritual and a symbolic part of our gathering. It is significant to realize the gifts are brought *through* the assembly indicating these are from the people. This also indicates each individual is making a gift of themselves to be transformed with the bread and wine, just as Christ gifted himself to the Father. Pope Benedict reminded us of this when he stated, "This humble and simple gesture is actually very significant: in the bread and wine that we bring to the altar, all creation is taken up by Christ the Redeemer to be transformed and presented to the Father" (*Sacramentum Caritatis,* # 47).

After receiving the bread and wine, the priest places them on the altar and then picks up the paten and says, "Blessed are you, Lord, God of all creation. Through your goodness we have this bread to offer, which earth has given and human hands have made. It will become for us the bread of life". This short prayer explicitly says what the collection and the procession have said implicitly.

Next, a small amount of water is added to the wine with the prayer: "By the mystery of this water and wine may we come to share in the divinity of Christ who humbled himself to share in our humanity." The water can be seen to symbolize the human nature of Jesus which is united in a mysterious way to his divine nature. The water may also symbolize ourselves who desire to be united with Jesus both in his humanity and in his divinity. The prayer recognizes that there is something of the divine as well as the human in each of us.

The priest then raises the chalice and prays, "Blessed are you, Lord, God of all creation. Through your goodness we have this wine to offer, fruit of the vine, and work of human hands. It will become our spiritual drink." If these prayers are said aloud, we respond, "Blessed be God forever." Again, this short prayer reinforces our praise for God. By presenting the bread and the wine to the Father and elevating them a little above the altar, we pray a brief prayer of praise taken from the Jewish tradition. Both prayers recognize the gifts have come to us through items grown from the earth and prepared by human hands.

What follows is a private prayer offered by the priest, humbly asking God to accept the people and sacrifice that will be offered. He prays, "With humble spirit and contrite heart may we be accepted by you, O Lord, and may our sacrifice in your sight this day be pleasing to you, Lord God." This prayer originates from the story of the three young men in the fiery furnace. Azariah offers this prayer from within the flames asking that the sacrifice of his very life be pleasing to God. The priest, mindful of his sins, offers his sufferings together with the gifts on the altar.

The priest washes his hands saying quietly, "Wash me, O Lord, from my iniquity and cleanse me from my sins." This washing of hands took place at different parts of the liturgy before it settled into its present location. With the increased use of incensing, it also serves a practical function of cleaning the hands of the priest after handling the censer.

The celebrant then prays, "Pray, brethren, that my sacrifice and yours may be acceptable to God, the almighty Father." Notice here the priest mentions two sacrifices, that of the priest and that of the people.

Finally, there is the prayer over the gifts. While the prayer varies, it will always mention in some form the gifts brought to the altar and pray for their and our transformation. We respond saying Amen to all that has happened from the collecting of the gifts to that present moment.

The preparation of the altar and gifts prepares us for the center and high point of the entire celebration, which is the Eucharistic Prayer, a prayer of thanksgiving and sanctification.

The Eucharistic Prayer

Celebrating the Eucharist is an act of thanksgiving and has its fullest expression in the Eucharistic Prayer. It is not just a prayer for the priest; rather it is a prayer for all the faithful. This prayer is the prayer of the baptized and ordained, and is offered in the presence of God, and has thanksgiving as its central focus.

The celebrant gathers not only the bread and the wine, but the substance of our lives and joins them to Christ's perfect sacrifice, offering them to the Father. The *General Instruction of the Roman Missal* (GIRM) makes this point very clearly: "The meaning of this Prayer is that the whole congregation of the faithful joins with Christ in confessing the great deeds of God and in the offering of Sacrifice" (GIRM, # 78).

In all of the Eucharistic Prayers, the priest associates the assembly with himself in the prayer he addresses in the name of the entire community to the Father through Jesus in the Holy Spirit: *It is truly right and just, our duty and our salvation, always and everywhere to give you thanks, Lord holy Father almighty and eternal God* (Roman Missal).

The priest offers the Eucharistic Prayer in the first person plural, for example, "Therefore, O Lord, *we* humbly implore you." This "we" signifies that all the baptized present at the Eucharistic celebration make the sacrificial offering in union with Christ and pray the Eucharistic Prayer in union with him.

It is worship offered to the Father by Christ as it was at the moment of his Passion, death, and Resurrection, but now it is offered through the priest acting in the person of Christ and it is offered as well by all of us who are part of Christ's Body, the Church.

The *General Instruction of the Roman Missal* #79 provides the following summary of the main elements of the Eucharistic Prayer:

a) The *thanksgiving* (expressed especially in the Preface), in which the priest, in the name of the whole of the holy people, glorifies God the Father and gives thanks to him for the whole work of salvation or for some particular aspect of it, according to the varying day, festivity, or time of year.
b) The *acclamation,* by which the whole congregation, joining with the heavenly powers, sings the *Sanctus (Holy, Holy, Holy).* This acclamation, which constitutes part of the Eucharistic Prayer itself, is pronounced by all the people with the priest.
c) The *epiclesis,* in which, by means of particular invocations, the church implores the power of the Holy Spirit that the gifts offered by human hands be consecrated, that is, become Christ's Body and Blood, and that the unblemished sacrificial Victim to be consumed in Communion may be for the salvation of those who will partake of it.
d) The *institution narrative and consecration,* by which, by means of the words and actions of Christ, that sacrifice is effected which Christ himself instituted during the Last Supper, when he offered his Body and Blood under the species of bread and wine, gave them to the Apostles to eat and drink, and leaving with the latter the command to perpetuate this same mystery.
e) The *anamnesis,* by which the Church, fulfilling the command that she received from Christ the Lord through the apostles, celebrates the memorial of Christ, recalling especially his blessed Passion, glorious Resurrection, and Ascension into heaven.
f) The *oblation,* by which, in this very memorial, the Church, in particular that gathered here and now, offers the unblemished sacrificial Victim in the Holy Spirit to the Father. The Church's intention, indeed, is that the faithful not only offer this unblemished sacrificial Victim but also learn to

offer their very selves, and so day by day to be brought, through the mediation of Christ, into unity with God and with each other, so that God may at last be all in all.

g) The *intercessions,* by which expression is given to the fact that the Eucharist is celebrated in communion with the whole Church, of both heaven and of earth, and that the oblation is made for her and for all her members, living and dead, who are called to participate in the redemption and salvation purchased by the Body and Blood of Christ.

h) The *concluding doxology,* by which the glorification of God is expressed and which is affirmed and concluded by the people's acclamation "*Amen.*"

The Eucharistic Prayer is the central prayer of the Mass; it is abundantly more than simply the Consecration. This prayer is one of thanksgiving and sanctification; the content of the words before and after the Consecration are rich in meaning and beyond ceremonial. This entire prayer is best realized as an entire narrative with a multiplicity of elements whose full meaning can only be understood in relationship to each other.

THE COMMUNION RITE

After the great Amen that closes the Eucharistic Prayer, the Communion Rite of the Mass begins. As we prepare to share Holy Communion, the faithful prays the Our Father. The *General Instruction of the Roman Missal* (GIRM) teaches, "In the Lord's Prayer a petition is made for daily bread, which for Christians means principally the Eucharistic Bread, and entreating also purification from sin, so that what is holy may in truth be given to the holy" (GIRM, # 81).

Following the Lord's Prayer, the celebrant prays that the assembly may be delivered from every evil as they await the coming of Christ. This prayer (Deliver us, Lord, we pray, from every evil and grant us peace in our days) is an insertion which we call an embolism.

This embolism is concluded with a doxology that is very well-known today among Protestant Christians (For the kingdom, the power, and the glory are yours, now and forever). The invitation from the priest, the actual Our Father prayer, the embolism, and the Doxology are all segments of The Lord's Prayer.

The Rite of Peace follows. In this prayer something very important occurs. The celebrant up to this part of the Mass either addresses his words to those gathered or to God the Father. Now he is addressing a prayer directly to Christ. This change occurs because we just prayed the Eucharistic Prayer, which is one of thanksgiving and sanctification and where the transubstantiation occurred. The meaning of the Rite of Peace has two facets. The Church first asks the Lord for unity and peace for herself and our families; and secondly, the assembly shows their mutual concern and charity for each other.

The GIRM is clear on how we should offer the sign of peace to others: "It is appropriate that each person offer the sign of peace, in a sober manner, only to those who are nearest" (GIRM, # 82). Clearly it is not a time to high five those around us or attempt to interact with everyone near us. This is not mere human fraternity being exchanged; it is the peace of Christ that is exchanged.

The Fraction Rite occurs next. The celebrant breaks the consecrated bread as the people sing the "Lamb of God." He then puts a piece of the host into the chalice to signify the unity of the Body and Blood of the Lord in the work of salvation. He says quietly, "May this mingling of the Body and Blood of our Lord Jesus Christ bring eternal life to us who receive it" (Roman Missal, # 129).

The gesture of breaking bread done by Jesus at the Last Supper became the name for the entire Eucharistic action during apostolic times. Back in the time of the apostles, the tearing of an actual loaf of bread recalled the suffering of Jesus, and the sharing of it helped them recall the Last Supper. The action served the practical purpose of allowing the many to eat from the one loaf, but it actually held much deeper meaning.

Before receiving Holy Communion, the celebrant acknowledges his unworthiness to receive the gift of the Eucharist by praying a silent prayer so that he may fruitfully receive the Body and Blood of the Lord.

He then invites all gathered to make a statement of faith by showing them the host above the chalice saying, "Behold the Lamb of God." The worshipping community expresses their unworthiness and prays for healing, "Lord, I am not worthy to receive you." This response by the assembly comes from the story of the healing of the centurion's slave (Luke 7:1–10).

While the celebrant receives Holy Communion, the Communion Song begins. The unity of voices echoes the unity the Eucharist brings. Then the people come forward. The faithful approach the minister, bowing their head in reverence and are then offered Communion with the formula "The Body of Christ" or "The Blood of Christ." The person receiving responds with the Hebrew word "Amen."

Holy Communion is distributed under both the form of bread and wine. The GIRM is clear, "For in this form, the sign of the Eucharistic banquet is more clearly evident" (GIRM, # 281).

After all have received, the priest, deacon, or instituted acolyte purify the sacred vessels. The Communion Song is completed so all can have a period of sacred silence for praise and thanksgiving of the Eucharist.

The Communion Rite ends with the prayer after Communion, which asks that the benefits of the Eucharist will remain active in our daily lives.

The Communion Rite is more than just about getting a host or drinking from the chalice. It involves a dying to the values of our world that are contrary to gospel values and to rise to a new way of life that is the very life of Jesus Christ. To receive Holy Communion is to hand ourselves over to allow Christ to consume us completely. It is in the Communion Rite that we commit ourselves to allow Christ to change us into him so that his way becomes our way.

The Concluding Rites

The Second Vatican Council was very clear in telling us that liturgy is important to our Christian life. The Constitution on the Sacred Liturgy (CSL) teaches us, "The liturgy is the summit toward which the activity of the Church is directed; at the same time it is the fount from which all the Church's power flows" (CSL, # 10). When we come to church to celebrate at Mass we follow what the Catechism calls a "fundamental structure which has been preserved throughout the centuries down to our own day" (Catechism of the Catholic Church, #1346). This structure is really one act of worship in four very distinctive phases.

Here is a very brief overview of the first three sections of the Mass. The Introductory Rites serve as a preparation for and introduction to the Eucharistic Sacrifice. The Liturgy of the Word is where Sacred Scripture is proclaimed, responded to, and explained. This section of the Mass helps to form the parish community into the body of Christ. The Liturgy of the Eucharist has two high points; the first is the Eucharistic Prayer and the second is the sharing of Holy Communion. The other elements of this section of the Mass prepare for and flow from these important sections. The Concluding Rites send us forth into the world to live out what we have celebrated.

The Concluding Rite of the Mass is very brief, yet it sends us out to be the Body and Blood of Christ for each other and the world. The *General Instruction of the Roman Missal* (GIRM) states, "The concluding rites consist of: a) brief announcements, if they are necessary; b) the priest's greeting and blessing, which on certain days and occasions is enriched and expressed in the prayer over the people or another more solemn formula; c) the dismissal of the people by the deacon or the priest so that each member goes out to do good works, while praising and blessing God; d) the kissing of the altar by the priest and the deacon, followed by a profound bow to the altar by the priest, the deacon, and the other ministers" (GIRM, #90). That sounds like a lot is going on, but actually, the entire rite takes up about one page of the Roman Missal when the priest uses the normal standard form. It is interesting to note that what we call the Mass comes from the Latin words of the dismissal text "Ite Missa est," which means "Go, the Mass is ended." The Latin word "Missa" is related to the word "missio," which is the root of the English word "mission." This reminds us that the liturgy does not simply come to an end. Those assembled are sent forth to bring the fruits of the Eucharist to the world. At the very end of the Mass we are given a commissioning to go into the world and preach the gospel.

Following the announcements, if indeed any are to be made, the celebrant greets the people and then blesses those assembled. He has the option of using the simple (standard) form or a more extensive version. In every case, the blessing always follows the Trinitarian form which is "May Almighty God bless you, the Father, and the Son, and the Holy Spirit" (Roman Missal, #41). On certain days or occasions, this blessing is preceded by a more solemn formula of blessing or by a prayer over the people.

The Roman Missal has an entire section of the Missal dedicated to blessings at the end of Mass and prayers over the people. The first section contains blessings and prayers for the different liturgical times of the year, including Advent, Christmas, the beginning of the New Year, the Epiphany, the Passion of the Lord, Easter, the Ascension of the Lord, the Holy Spirit, and ordinary time. The next section contains prayers and blessings for the celebration of saints. These include the Blessed Virgin Mary, Saints Peter and Paul, the Apostles, and all saints.

When a bishop is giving the final blessing, he has an additional dialogue with the assembly. In a Pontifical Mass, the dialogue unfolds according to the Ceremonial of Bishops as follows: The Bishop with his hands extended says, "The Lord be with you," everyone responds, "And with your spirit." The bishop then says, "*Blessed be the name of the Lord." All respond,* "Now and forever." (These two phrases come from Psalm 113 verse 2.) The bishop continues, "*Our help is in the name of the Lord," and the assembly answers,* "Who made heaven and earth." (This second set of phrases comes from Psalm 124 verse 8.)

After the priest's blessing, the deacon (when present) dismisses the people. The Roman Missal provides him with four options to choose from. They include "Go forth the mass is ended, Go and announce the Gospel of the Lord, Go in peace, glorifying the Lord by your life, Go in peace" (Roman Missal, #144). The people then reply, "Thanks be to God." Following the response of the people, the clergy venerate the altar just as they did at the beginning of the Mass. After making a profound bow with the ministers, the priest withdraws. The Concluding Rites of the Mass are truly very brief.

We come to Mass to offer our praise and thanks to God. Throughout the Eucharist, we gather together as God's holy people, are fed by the Liturgy of the Word and at the table of the Lord. The Concluding Rites send us forth to go back into our community, our families, and our workplace. We are dismissed from the Holy Sacrifice of the Mass with a commissioning to go back into the world, to do good works, and to praise and bless God. The Concluding Rites of the Mass help us to complete our act of worship in church, but lead us to continue our mission to be disciples of Jesus Christ in the world.

The Sacraments of the Catholic Church

Jesus' words and actions during his hidden life and public ministry were already salvific, for they anticipated the power of his Paschal mystery. They announced and prepared what he was going to give the Church when all was accomplished. The mysteries of Christ's life are the foundations of what he would henceforth dispense in the sacraments, through the ministers of his Church, for "what was visible in our Savior has passed over into his mysteries." (*Catechism of the Catholic Church: no 1115)*

The Sacrament of Baptism

The sacraments of the church are the principal means by which the faith of the church is built up and celebrated. The Catholic Church believes and teaches that by the sacraments and the full participation of God's holy people, worship is offered to God through Jesus in union of the Holy Spirit. Baptism is the gateway to the other sacraments and to the life of grace. "Baptism incorporates us into Christ, and forms us into God's people. This first sacrament pardons all our sins, rescues us from the power of darkness, and brings us to the dignity of adopted children, a new creation through water and the Holy Spirit" (Rite of Baptism for Children, #2). All of the sacraments make visible an invisible reality. We experience this in the sacrament of baptism in the words of the church and in the physical signs and rituals used to express our experience of God and his grace in our lives.

There are many symbols present at a celebration of Baptism: the sign of the cross, the words prayed, water, oil, a white garment, a baptismal candle, the minister, parents, godparents, and the assembly. The sign of the cross that is traced on the forehead of the person being baptized expresses the mystery of the cross, which is at the heart of our faith. The sacramental words "I baptize you in the name of the Father, and of the Son, and of the Holy Spirit," are prayed while the water is poured over the head or the person is immersed. These words reveal that God in the Trinity is the source of life. The immersion into the blest water or the pouring of the blest water reminds us that we die with Christ to conquer sin and rise with him so we might enter into new life. The newly baptized is anointed with sacred chrism, which is a mixture of olive oil and balsam, showing that the Holy Spirit dwells within the heart of this new Christian. It's also a sign of being anointed to a mission to live and love as Jesus lived. The white garment worn after the person is baptized expresses that the person has "put on Christ," taking on a new identity as a child of God; becoming a new creation. The baptismal candle, which is lit from the Paschal (Easter) candle, represents the light of Christ, a light to guide the new believer throughout his or her life.

The ordinary (normal) minister of the sacrament of baptism is the bishop, a priest, or deacon. In every celebration of the sacrament of baptism, they act in the Church in the name of Christ and the power of the Holy Spirit" (Rite of Baptism for Children, #11). The Catechism teaches us, "In case of necessity (meaning a dire emergency), anyone, even a non-baptized person, with the required intention, can baptize, by using the Trinitarian baptismal formula" (Catechism of the Catholic Church, #1256).

The parents of a child, moved by their own faith, are to be the first teachers of the faith to their child. During the celebration they publically ask that their child be baptized, they sign their child with the sign of the cross after the celebrant, they make a profession of faith, they carry their child to the waters of baptism, they hold the lighted candle, and are blessed with prayers formulated for them. Those parents who seek a baptism of their infant or young child must attend a baptismal workshop, so they fully understand what they are undertaking. The godparents (for a child) or a sponsor (for an adult) assist in presenting the one to be baptized. They are to help the one being baptized to live the Christian life. A question that sometimes arises is, "If parents choose not to have their child baptized, may another family member, such as the grandparents, present the child for baptism?" The answer is no, since at least one of the parents has to agree to the baptism because the parents are the first teachers of the faith.

The qualification for serving as a godparent or sponsor, according the Canon Law, are as follows: the person must be designated by the one to be baptized (or by the parent in the case of an infant); must be sixteen years of age or older (the local bishop may establish a different age), be a Catholic, confirmed and who has received the Eucharist, and is living a life consistent with the faith. Godparents cannot be a parent of the one to be baptized. A baptized person who is not a Catholic may serve as a witness to the baptism with a Catholic sponsor (Code of Canon Law #872–874). The people of God also play an important role in the celebration. They are called to live the gospel message, so the one who has been baptized has others on the journey of faith to follow.

The rite for the celebration of Baptism consists of the following main sections: the reception of the child, which includes opening questions to parents and godparents followed by the signing with the cross; the Liturgy of the Word; the Prayer of Exorcism and Anointing before baptism; the blessing of the water in the font; the renewal of Baptismal promises followed by the actual Baptism; the anointing with the sacred chrism; the clothing with the white Baptismal garment; the receiving of the lighted candle; and finally the blessing and dismissal of those assembled.

Within weeks of Jesus's Resurrection, the apostles were preaching the Gospel to people and were baptizing them in Jesus's name. Since then, Baptism has been the ordinary (normal) means of becoming a member of the Church. Catholics are not born, they are made—baptism is the process by which we incorporate people into our worshipping community.

THE SACRAMENT OF CONFIRMATION

The Sacrament of Confirmation is the last of three initiation rites for Catholics, the other two being *Baptism* and Eucharist. Through the Sacrament of Confirmation, bishops share the gift of the Holy Spirit upon the baptized faithful, just as the apostles received the Holy Spirit at Pentecost.

Confirmation deepens our baptismal life; it calls us to be witnesses of Jesus Christ in all that we do and with all we encounter. We receive the message of faith at Baptism, and are strengthened and nourished by the Eucharist. "Confirmation perfects Baptismal grace; it is the sacrament which gives the Holy Spirit in order to root us more deeply in the divine filiation, incorporate us more firmly into Christ, strengthen our bond with the Church, associate us more closely with her mission, and help us bear witness to the Christian faith in words accompanied by deeds" (*Catechism of the Catholic Church, #1316*).

The Sacrament of Confirmation has had a long, complex history. Originally, confirmation was not distinct from Baptism. However, but in the fourth and fifth centuries, the rites following Baptism came to be particularly associated with the gift of the Holy Spirit. By the fifth century, Roman practice was beginning to separate Baptism and a post-baptismal anointing from a laying on of hands and a second anointing, which were reserved to the bishop. Confirmation became a separate sacrament from this laying on of hands and second anointing. Today, the celebration of the Rite of Christian Initiation of Adults reemphasizes the connection between Baptism and Confirmation.

Those to be confirmed are assisted by a sponsor, who present the candidate to the bishop, then following the liturgy, help the newly confirmed to live their baptismal promises fully. "It is desirable that the godparent at baptism also be the sponsor at Confirmation" (*The Order of Confirmation, #5*), so that the link between Baptism and Confirmation is more clearly expressed. The option of choosing a different sponsor for Confirmation is also allowed.

The qualifications for serving as a sponsor are found in the Code of Canon Law. Canon 893 #1 states that Confirmation sponsors should meet the requirements of baptismal sponsor. That means a sponsor must be at least sixteen years old, unless another age is set by the bishop, must be a Catholic who has received all three sacraments of initiation and who leads a life in harmony with the Catholic faith. The sponsor must not be bound by any penalty of the Church and must not be the parent of the person to be confirmed.

The bishop is the ordinary (normal) minister of Confirmation "so that there will be a more evident relationship to the first pouring forth of the Holy Spirit on Pentecost" (Rite of Confirmation, #7). A priest who baptizes a person who is not an infant or admits one already baptized into full communion with the Catholic Church also has the faculty to confirm. A priest may also confirm a person who is in danger of imminent death.

The preparation for Confirmation focuses the candidate toward a more intimate union with Christ and a better understanding of the Holy Spirit so that the person will be more able to assume the apostolic responsibilities of Christian life. To receive Confirmation one must be in a state of grace. Confirmation, like Baptism, imprints a spiritual mark or indelible character on the Christian's soul; for this reason a person receives this sacrament only once.

Confirmation usually takes place within Mass so that the connection between the Eucharist and this Sacrament with all of Christian initiation may become clearer. After the Gospel, the candidates are presented to the bishop; he gives a homily and questions those to be confirmed through the renewal of their baptismal promises. After asking all to pray for those to be confirmed and a period of silence, the bishop lays hands over all to be confirmed and prays the following: "Almighty God, Father of our Lord Jesus Christ, who brought these servants to new birth by water and the Holy Spirit, freeing them from sin; send upon them, O Lord, the Holy Spirit, the Paraclete; give them the spirit of wisdom and understanding, the spirit of counsel and fortitude, the spirit of knowledge and piety; fill them with the spirit of fear of the Lord. Through Christ our Lord" (*The Order of Confirmation, #25*).

Each of those to be confirmed then goes to the bishop. The sponsor places their right hand on the shoulder of the candidate and the candidate's confirmation name is said. The bishop dips the tip of his right thumb in the Sacred Chrism, makes the sign of the cross on the forehead of the one to be confirmed, and says, "Be sealed with the gift of the Holy Spirit." The newly confirmed replies, "Amen." The bishop adds, "Peace be with you" and the newly confirmed says, "And with your Spirit." Mass continues as normal with the Universal Prayer.

Baptism, Eucharist, and Confirmation together constitute the "sacraments of Christian initiation." It is through the Sacrament of Confirmation that the baptized are more perfectly bound to the Church and are enriched with a special strength of the Holy Spirit.

THE SACRAMENT OF EUCHARIST

The word *Eucharist* refers to more than the Body and Blood of Christ. It comes from the Greek word meaning, "To give thanks." The Eucharist is no mere symbol, but is in fact the true body and blood of Jesus Christ, which has the ability to transform our hearts and minds to be more like him. The Catholic Church stresses that the Eucharist is not a private prayer or a beautiful spiritual experience; it's not simply a commemoration of what Jesus did in the Last Supper. It is a memorial, a gesture, that actualizes and makes present the event of the death and resurrection of Jesus.

The Catechism of the Catholic Church (CCC) teaches, "By the consecration, the transubstantiation of the bread and wine into the Body and Blood of Christ is brought about. Under the consecrated species of bread and wine Christ himself, living and glorious, is present in a true, real, and substantial manner: his Body and his Blood, with his soul and his divinity" (CCC, #1413). The essential signs of the Eucharistic sacrament are wheat bread and grape wine, on which the blessing of the Holy Spirit is invoked and the priest pronounces the words of consecration spoken by Jesus during the Last Supper: "This is my body which will be given up for you. This is the cup of my blood."

In the early church the term Eucharist designated not only the bread and wine, but also the ritual of worship. The Eucharist is like a many faceted diamond. The Catechism offers nine different names for Eucharist: "The Lord's Supper, The Breaking of the Bread, The Eucharistic Assembly, The Memorial of the Lord's Passion and Resurrection, The Holy Sacrifice, The Holy and Divine Liturgy, Holy Communion and Holy Mass" (CCC, #1329–1332).

The Eucharist is the source and summit of Christian life. Vatican II provides us with our understanding of the Eucharist. The documents have shifted our attention from the Blessed Sacrament as an object of worship to the entire liturgy as an act of worship; a belief in real presence of Christ in the Blessed Sacrament; and has emphasized the presence of Christ in the church and in the entire Eucharistic liturgy.

Life in Christ has its foundation in the Eucharistic banquet. When we receive the Body and Blood of Jesus, we proclaim to each other the Good News of our salvation that the risen Christ is in our midst. Celebrating the Eucharist renews the life of grace we received at Baptism. The spiritual nourishment helps us on our daily pilgrimage on earth. When we are near the moment of death, we will receive the Holy Eucharist for our journey toward heaven. This final communion here on earth is called viaticum, meaning food for the journey. The Eucharist strengthens our charity toward others. Receiving Communion is a communal act, as we process toward the one table of the Lord, we are united to all the faithful, not just in our parish or diocese, but to the entire Church.

Bishops, priests, and deacons are considered the ordinary ministers of Holy Communion. When the size of the community requires it, the celebrant may be assisted by lay ministers who have received spiritual, theological, and practical preparation to serve their worshipping community with reverence and knowledge. During Mass, Holy Communion is distributed under both the form of bread and wine. The *General Instruction of the Roman Missal* (GIRM) is clear: "For in this form, the sign of the Eucharistic banquet is more clearly evident" (GIRM, #281). It is very important to have the correct attitude and posture when receiving communion. The faithful approach the minister, bowing their head in reverence and then is offered Communion with the formula "The Body of Christ" or "The Blood of Christ." The person receiving responds with the Hebrew word "Amen." When receiving communion, we should be guided by the words of St. Cyril of Jerusalem who taught the importance of placing your left hand as a throne beneath your right.

The National Conference of Catholic Bishops approved the following guidelines on the reception of Communion: "As Catholics, we fully participate in the celebration of the Eucharist when we receive Holy Communion. We are encouraged to receive Communion devoutly and frequently. In order to be properly disposed to receive Communion, participants should not be conscious of grave sin and normally should have fasted for one hour. A person who is conscious of grave sin is not to receive the Body and Blood of the Lord without prior sacramental confession except for a grave reason where there is no opportunity for confession. In this case, the person is to be mindful of the obligation to make an act of perfect contrition, including the intention of confessing as soon as possible (Code of Canon Law, #916). A frequent reception of the Sacrament of Penance is encouraged for all."

The fruits of Holy Communion are many. Holy Communion increases our union with Christ and with his Church. It preserves and renews the life of grace received at Baptism and Confirmation and makes us grow in love for others. It strengthens us in charity, wipes away venial sins, and preserves us from mortal sin in the future.

THE SACRAMENT OF HOLY ORDERS

The sacrament of Holy Orders is the sacrament through which the mission entrusted by Christ to his apostles continues to be exercised in the Church. It includes the three degrees of the sacrament which are episcopate (bishop), presbyterate (priest), and diaconate (deacon). Candidates for priesthood ordination, also called *ordinands*, receive the Sacrament of Holy Orders in culmination of several years of rigorous study and spiritual development. This formation contains human, spiritual, academic (intellectual), and pastoral formation, plus a full schedule of spiritual activities and spiritual direction and retreats.

The ordination ceremony of a priest includes a variety of rituals, which are packed with abundant meaning. The ordination ceremony includes various rituals that are rich in significance. The Ordination Rite of Priest begins after the Gospel with *The Election of the Candidates*. The rite consists of designated priests replying to the bishop's questions by informing him that there are no doubts about the candidates for priesthood.

After the homily, *The Promises of the Elect (and Promise of Obedience)* occurs. This is where the ordinands resolve to carry out their office in accord with the mind of Christ, the Church, and under the direction of the bishop. During the *Litany of Supplication*, the candidates lie prostrate on the floor and the Litany of the Saints is sung. The act of lying prostrate symbolizes his unworthiness for the office to be assumed and his dependence upon God and the prayers of the Christian community. This Litany asks for the intercession of the saints in order that God may look favorably upon those to be ordained.

Next the bishop continues with *The Laying on of Hands*. With his hands extended over the candidate, the bishop says the great "Prayer of Consecration," asking God to grant the candidate "the dignity of the priesthood." The action of "Laying on of Hands" and the "Prayer of Consecration" are the heart of the Ordination Rite and confer the grace of ministerial priesthood. By this ritual the ordaining bishop and the other priests invoke the Holy Spirit to come down upon the one to be ordained, giving him a sacred character and setting him apart for the designated ministry.

Immediately after, the *Investiture of the New Priests* begins with the placing of a priestly stole and chasuble on the newly ordained. These vestments associated with a priest have symbolic meaning. The stole symbolizes the authority and responsibility to serve in imitation of Christ. The chasuble is the principle garment of the priest celebrating the Eucharist.

Once the priest is vested with his chasuble, *The Anointing of Hands and the Handing Over of the Bread and Wine* occur. The ordained come forward one by one and kneel before the bishop. He then takes the oil of catechumens and anoints their hands, tracing a cross across both palms. The bishop then closes or joins together the hands of the ordained and binds the consecrated hands together with a white cloth. This cloth is usually later given after his first Mass to the mother of the priest (who is in turn buried with the cloth to present at the gates of heaven acknowledging she gave her son to God). Anointing with oil stems from the Old Testament and indicates that someone or something is being set apart for a sacred task or duty. The anointing of the hands signifies that the hands of the newly ordained priest are being prepared for the sacred duties and vessels, which will be part of the priestly ministry. The bishop says as he anoints the hands, "The Father anointed our Lord Jesus Christ through the power of the Holy Spirit. May Jesus preserve you to sanctify the Christian people and to offer sacrifice to God." The anointing of hands symbolizes the priests' distinctive participation in Christ's priesthood.

The handing over of the bread and wine, placed in the hands of the newly ordained priest, points to their duty of presiding at the celebration of the Holy Eucharist and of following Christ crucified. The Eucharist is at the heart of the priesthood and this ritual highlights the importance of celebrating the Eucharist in the life of the priest and its meaning, as seen in the words which are spoken by the bishop: "Accept from the holy people of God the gifts to be offered to him. Know what you are doing, and imitate the mystery you celebrate; model your life on the mystery of the Lord's cross."

Finally, the bishop and all of the priests present give the *kiss of peace* (it usually is a full shoulder embrace) to the newly ordained priests. This is to seal their admittance to the rank of coworkers with the other members of the local clergy. The other priests welcome the newly ordained as a fellow brother in their shared ministry. The Mass then continues with the Liturgy of the Eucharist.

The sacrament of Holy Orders is conferred by the laying on of hands followed by a solemn prayer of consecration asking God to grant the ordinand the graces of the Holy Spirit required for his ministry.

THE SACRAMENT OF MATRIMONY

The sacrament of Matrimony is one of the seven sacraments of the Catholic Church. It is considered a sacrament of vocation. The Church has a rich theology concerning this sacrament. It began with God himself, who entered into a lasting covenant relationship with his people. Sacred Scripture begins with the creation of man and woman made in the image and likeness of God. In the Book of Genesis, we read that man and woman were created for one another: "It is not good for the man to be alone. I will make a helper suited to him" (Genesis 2:18). This intimate bond, created by God, shows the unbreakable union of their two lives, since as scripture states, "They are no longer two, but one flesh" (Genesis 2:24).

We read in the Gospels how Jesus brought dignity, blessings, and joy when he attended the wedding at Cana. There he changed water into wine and by doing so foreshadowed the new covenant of love. The Code of Canon Law (Canon) teaches, "The marriage covenant, by which a man and a woman establish between themselves a partnership of their whole life, and which of its own very nature is ordered to the well-being of the spouses and to the procreation and upbringing of children, has, between the baptized, been raised by Christ the Lord to the dignity of a sacrament. Consequently, a valid marriage contract cannot exist between baptized persons without its being by that very fact a sacrament" (Canon, #1055).

In the sacrament of Matrimony, Christian spouses participate in the love of Christ and the Church. God the Father, Son, and Holy Spirit are united in a community of love, just as a husband and wife are united in their community of love. Matrimony is not just a private relationship between a man and a woman, but is actually a *per-*

sonal relationship lived out within society. The Sacrament of Matrimony is a covenantal union. Married love is one of the images of God's love for all humankind. The Catechism of the Catholic Church (CCC) teaches, "The entire Christian life bears the mark of the spousal love of Christ and the Church... Christian marriage in its turn becomes an efficacious sign, the sacrament of the covenant of Christ and the Church. Since it signifies and communicates grace, marriage between baptized persons is a true sacrament of the New Covenant" (CCC, #1617).

The Catholic Church wants couples to be well-prepared before they enter into their union. The church offers marriage preparation to help couples develop a better understanding of this sacred sacrament, to gain wisdom into themselves as individuals and as a couple, and to help them evaluate and deepen their readiness to live the married state. There are a variety of marriage preparation programs available depending on the parish and the diocese. The topics usually covered include the meaning of matrimony as a sacrament, the importance of faith and prayer, the roles each person will undertake in marriage, the importance of conflict resolution and communication, parenthood and children, finances and natural family planning.

Catholics believe that marriage is a gift from God. The church teaches that the sacrament unites husband and wife in a mutual and faithful love, the couple should be open to children, it calls the couple to be a witness of Christ's love to all they encounter and it is a way of holiness for the couple. The three basic requirements for a valid Catholic wedding are the couple must be capable of being married, which means they must be a woman and a man who are free of any impediment that would prevent marriage, the couple must give their consent to be married during the rite, and they must be married according to the laws of the Church.

In the Rite of Matrimony, the Questions before the Consent are an important part of a Catholic wedding ceremony. These questions occur right after the homily. It is here where the priest or deacon asks the bride and groom a series of questions immediately before they exchange their consent and are married. As the Order of Celebrating Matrimony (OCM) explains, these questions involve the couple's "freedom of choice, fidelity to each other, and the acceptance and upbringing of children" (OCM, #60). While they are asked the questions together, each person must answer the questions individually. It is a very important and solemn moment, as bride and groom vow before God and the worshipping community their intention to undertake with the grace of God the vocation that is a lifelong marriage. The Catechism states, "The Church holds the exchange of consent between the spouses to be the indispensable element that 'makes the marriage'" (CCC, #1626). If consent is lacking, there is no marriage. The Catechism continues, "From a valid marriage arises a bond between the spouses which by its very nature is perpetual and exclusive; furthermore, in a Christian marriage the spouses are strengthened and, as it were, consecrated for the duties and the dignity of their state by a special sacrament" (CCC, #1638).

God encountered his people with a covenant of love from the beginning of time. Jesus Christ is part of every Christian marriage. By the power of the Holy Spirit, the married couple receives the graces necessary to help each other get to heaven.

Following the Second Vatican Council, the church published a revised Rite of Marriage in Latin in 1969 and the official English translation was published in 1970. In 1991, a revised version of this Order of Marriage was published in Latin, but the English translation was delayed. Part of this delay was a result of a different set of translation principles that emphasize a more direct translation from the official Latin. This was mandated by the Vatican's 2001 document *Liturgiam Authenticam*.

The *Order of Celebrating Matrimony* (*Ordo celebandi Matrimonium*) was canonically approved for use by the United States Conference of Bishops on November 12, 2013, and was confirmed for the Apostolic See by decree of the Congregation for Divine Worship and the Discipline of the Sacraments on June 29, 2015. The *Order of Celebrating Matrimony* became obligatory as of December 30, 2016.

There are many new elements in this Second Typical Edition. This revised rite has a new name. It is now referred to as the *Order of Celebrating Matrimony* (OCM). The bishops felt the word "matrimony" has a more sacred connotation than "marriage." They thought the change was especially important in the American context, where we've seen attempts to redefine what marriage even means. Overall, as with the current Roman Missal, even the same prayers will have a different sound to them because of the different set of translation principles employed.

The Praenotanda (the Introduction of the ritual book) offers clergy, and liturgists a deeper exposition of the Church's theology of marriage. This expanded introduction now contains forty-four paragraphs instead of the original eighteen. These paragraphs include material concerning: the importance and dignity of the Sacrament of Matrimony, the duties and ministries of the bishop, the pastor, the deacon, the engaged couple, and the lay people who will help in the spiritual preparation of the couple. The entire Christian community "should cooperate to bear witness to the faith and to be a sign to the world of Christ's love" (OCM, #26).

The Entrance Rites are expanded providing the priest or deacon a choice of two introductory addresses to help all present dispose themselves more appropriately for the celebration (OCM, #52). The Penitential Act (Lord, have mercy) is omitted and the Gloria will now be always included (even during Advent and Lent) when marriage is celebrated in the context of Mass. The set of Scripture Readings has been expanded offering one additional Old Testament and four additional New Testament readings.

The priest or deacon now has an expanded prayer as part of the "Reception of Consent." It invokes Abraham, Isaac, Jacob, and even Adam and Eve. Following the consent, the whole assembly is invited to respond with an acclamation. The celebrant will say, "Let us bless the Lord" and all present will respond, "Thanks be to God." There is now a prayer for the couple as part of Eucharistic Prayer I, II, and III. The four nuptial blessings now include an invocation (epiclesis) calling down the blessing of the Holy Spirit.

The Holy See also approved two adaptations, which are traditional marriage practices in many Hispanic cultures and have long been a part of Spanish language and Filipino Catholic weddings. These include the optional blessing and giving of the arras (coins) and the optional blessing and placing of the lazo or veil. These two adaptations were already approved for use in the United States in the Spanish ritual book since 2010, now with this Second Edition, the Vatican, at the request of the American bishops, allows their use in English language weddings as well.

The word *arras* literally means "pledge." Usually, the arras consists of coins symbolizing prosperity. The exchange of coins symbolizes the couple now shares everything. The lazo is a wedding garland to symbolize they are now bound together sacramentally. It usually consists of a double-looped rosary; one loop goes over the groom's shoulders and the other over the bride's with the cross hanging between them. The veil has its origins as a symbol of both a dying to one's past self and as a protection from danger. While the woman wears the veil, it is placed over the shoulder of the man and oftentimes the lazo helps to hold it in place.

By the Sacrament of Matrimony, Christian spouses signify and participate in the mystery of unity and fruitful love between Christ and the Church. The *Order of Celebrating Matrimony* has been revised in order that this richer rite would more clearly signify the grace of the sacrament and the responsibilities of the married couple.

THE SACRAMENT OF RECONCILIATION

The Sacrament of Reconciliation, also called Penance or Confession, is considered by the Church to be a sacrament of healing. This sacrament should be seen within the context of conversion from sin and a turning back to God. This is true, because sin harms our relationship with God and damages our communion with the Church. Conversion of heart is the beginning of our journey back to God. Liturgically this happens in the celebration of the Sacrament.

We get this invitation for repentance throughout the liturgical year, but especially throughout the holy seasons of Advent and Lent. We hear in Sacred Scripture, for example, through the writings of the prophets of the Old Testament, from John the Baptist, and by Jesus himself for all people to return to God and away from sin. Throughout his public ministry, the Lord exhorted people to repentance. Jesus welcomed and healed sinners and reconciled them to the Father. "Our Savior Jesus Christ, when he gave to his apostles and their successors power to forgive sins, instituted in his Church the sacrament of penance" (Rite of Penance, #2).

In the sacrament of penance, the faithful obtain from the mercy of God, pardon for their sins, and are also reconciled with the Church. In the Sacrament of Reconciliation, we confess our sins to God through his minister, the priest, who absolves us in the name of Christ. Within the liturgy of the sacrament, three elements are required from the penitent (the person confessing) for the forgiveness of sins to occur, they are Contrition, confession, and satisfaction or Penance (Rite of Penance, #6).

Contrition is having a sincere sorrow for offending God; this is really the most important act of the penitent. In fact, there can be no forgiveness of sin if we do not have sorrow and a firm resolve not to repeat our sin. In the confession section, the person who has sinned confronts their sins by speaking about them to the priest. The satisfaction part of the rite is where an important part of the healing occurs. This is where the priest gives the penitent their penance in reparation for one's sins.

In the prayer of absolution the priest speaks the words by which "God, the Father of Mercies" reconciles a sinner to himself through the merits of the cross. It is here that God grants pardon and peace to the person who in the sacramental confession showed their change of heart. The Sacrament of Penance reconciles us with God. "The whole power of the sacrament of Penance consists in restoring us to God's grace and joining us with him in an intimate friendship" (Catechism of the Catholic Church, #1468). The celebration concludes with the priest dismissing the person to "go in peace."

Holy Mother Church offers us four different rites of celebration: three are sacramental and one is non-sacramental. The Rite for Reconciliation of Individual Penitents is the most common sacramental form. This is the individual rite celebrated each week with individuals. The rite begins with the priest welcoming the penitent and addressing the person with friendly words (Rite of Penance, #16). Then the penitent makes the sign of the cross and the priest invites the person to have trust in God and his mercy. There could also be a reading from sacred Scripture at this point in the rite. The confession of sins and the giving of the person their penance occurs next, followed by the penitent expressing sorrow for their sins. This can be done using their own words, reading Sacred Scripture or a prescribed formula, commonly known as an Act of Contrition. The priest will then extend his hands and pray the Prayer of Absolution.

The Rite of Reconciliation of Several Penitents with Individual Confession and Absolution is the second sacramental form, which is used for communal Penance services usually during Advent and Lent. The Rite for Reconciliation of Several Penitents with General Confession and Absolution is also called general absolution and is the third sacramental form. This is very rare and may be used only in extraordinary circumstances when the bishop authorizes it or practical needs require its use. General absolution is given only when the number of penitents is large and the danger of death is great, or in circumstances such as natural disasters, or during wartime situations. When general absolution is given, the penitents are given absolution as a group without confessing their sins to the priest, with the understanding that they will go to confession at the earliest opportunity. The non-sacramental form is really just a prayer service in which those gathered acknowledge their sins and pray for forgiveness and renewal. This "penance service" does not involve sacramental confession, so there is no absolution or the remission of sins.

The Church recommends that a person go regularly to confession, even if only for venial sins. This is because "the regular confession of our venial sins helps us from our consciences, fight against evil tendencies, let ourselves be healed by Christ and progress in the life of the Spirit" (Catechism of the Catholic Church, # 1458). The sacrament of Reconciliation frees us from sins and also challenges us to have the same kind of compassion and forgiveness for those who sin against us.

The Sacrament of Anointing of the Sick

The Sacrament of Anointing of the Sick helps unite those who are suffering with Jesus's saving and healing power. From ancient times in the liturgical traditions of both East and West, we have testimonies to the practice of anointing the sick with blessed oil. In the Epistle of St. James, we are instructed, "Is any one among you sick? Let him bring in the presbyters [priests] of the church, and let them pray over him, anointing him with oil in the name of the Lord. And the prayer of faith will save the sick person, and the Lord will raise him up, and if he be in sin, they shall be forgiven him" (James 5:14–15). Through this sacrament, people receive forgiveness for their sins and comfort in their suffering; they are restored in spirit and sometimes they even experience the return of physical health.

The Sacrament of Anointing of the Sick is a sacrament of healing; it is no longer known as extreme unction or last rites. Before the Second Vatican Council this sacrament was celebrated when a person was near death, hence, the term last rites.

The Catechism of the Catholic Church (CCC) instructs us, "The proper time for receiving this holy anointing has certainly arrived when the believer begins to be in danger of death because of illness or old age. Each time a Christian falls seriously ill, he may receive the Anointing of the Sick, and also when, after he has received it, the illness worsens" (CCC, #1528–1529). A careful judgment about the serious nature of the illness is sufficient.

The Sacrament of Anointing of the Sick is not to be celebrated whenever you get a sore throat or just slice your finger cutting up some cucumbers. Surgery or other serious procedures that will be held in a hospital, even if the person is young, makes it an appropriate time to receive the sacrament. Whenever someone is diagnosed with a long term or serious illness or as a person experiences some type of health issues related to old age, the priest should be called to celebrate the sacrament.

Celebrating the Sacrament of Anointing of the Sick is a prayer for healing not only for one's physical body, but also for a person's spiritual health and to be able to handle the burden associated with illness. As Catholics, we are called to unite our pains and sufferings with the pains and sufferings of Christ. When the Sacrament of Anointing of the Sick is conferred, the hoped for effect is that, if it is God's will, the person will be physically healed of their illness. Even if there is no physical healing, celebrating the sacrament allows for a spiritual healing by which the sick person receives the Holy Spirit's gift of courage and peace to deal with the difficulties that accompany the frailty of old age or any serious illness.

In addition to anointing, the person is often offered Holy Communion. When a person is dying, this Holy Communion is called viaticum, meaning food for the journey. For a dying person, the sacrament is a preparation for passing over to eternal life. At the beginning of life, a person receives the initiation sacraments of Baptism, Confirmation, and Eucharist. Near the end of their life they receive the Sacraments of Penance, the Anointing of the Sick, and the Eucharist as viaticum which constitute the sacraments that prepare them for their heavenly homeland. They are the sacraments that complete our earthly pilgrimage.

The celebration of the sacrament can happen at Mass or outside of Mass, it can be celebrated at a person's home, in a hospital, or a nursing home. While the sacrament is often administered individually, the church encourages celebrating it with a community of people, since like all the sacraments it is a liturgical and communal celebration.

Only a priest can administer the sacrament. The oil he uses is olive oil blessed by the bishop at the Chrism Mass during Holy Week. In the Rite of the Anointing of the Sick #141, the priest anoints the sick person on the forehead, saying, "Through this holy anointing may the Lord in his love and mercy help you with the grace of the

Holy Spirit." He also anoints the sick person on the hands, saying, "May the Lord who frees you from sin save you and raise you up."

The celebration of the Sacrament of Anointing of the Sick gives courage to those afflicted during difficult times. In the Prayer after the Anointing, the priest prays, "Father in heaven, through this holy anointing grant our brothers and sisters comfort in their suffering. When they are afraid, give them courage, when afflicted, give them patience, when dejected, afford them hope, and when alone, assure them of the support of your holy people" (Prayer after Anointing, #142 A).

Suffering is a part of life, but Jesus unites our suffering with his passion and death so that through our suffering we can participate in his saving and healing work. The Sacrament of Anointing of the Sick gives the grace of the Holy Spirit to those who are sick or who have the frailty of old age. The Rites of Anointing of the Sick are used by the Church to comfort the sick in times of anxiety.

THE LITURGICAL YEAR

During the liturgical year the Church unfolds the whole mystery of Christ, from his incarnation and birth through his passion, death, and resurrection to his ascension, the day of Pentecost, and the expectation of his coming in glory. In its celebration of these mysteries, the Church makes these sacred events present to the people of every age. (*Sacrosanctum Concilium: Constitution on the Sacred Liturgy: no. 102)*

ADVENT

The word *Advent* comes from the Latin word *adventus,* which means "arrival." The first Sunday of Advent will be the following weekend after the celebration of the Solemnity of Our Lord Jesus Christ, King of the Universe (Christ the King Sunday). In the midst of all the Christmas carols in the malls, and all the gift-buying and associated business, it's important to remember the two foci of this liturgical season.

The first calls us to celebrate God present among us right now. The incarnation of Jesus is a historical event and also an ongoing event. Christ is still taking on flesh and he is continually present through his body, the church. We must remember that in Christ we have a future also, which is Advent's second focus. Christ came to us at Bethlehem, now lives in us; he will come again in the fullness of time when he will judge the living and the dead. Advent is not considered a penitential season, but rather a period of devout and expectant delight (Universal Norms on the Liturgical Calendar, #39).

The liturgical color of the season is violet, but on the third Sunday of Advent we use rose-colored vestments and fabrics. The rose candle of our Advent wreath is lit. We call this Sunday "Gaudete Sunday," which is Latin for "Rejoice." The imagery of light occurs throughout the liturgical texts, so central to this motif is the Advent Wreath. This devotional practice contains live greenery made from evergreens and four candles, one for each week of the season. The Advent Wreath should not be placed on or near the altar. This follows the rubric from *The Book of Blessings* which states, "If it is to be placed in the sanctuary, the Advent Wreath is not to interfere with the celebration of the liturgy, obscure that altar, ambo or celebrants chair" (*Book of Blessings*, #1512).

Year A of the Sunday Lectionary will be proclaimed. It is the Gospel account according to St. Matthew. In this gospel, Jesus calls Peter "the Rock." Our Savior tells us Peter also holds the keys to the Kingdom of Heaven. This is the gospel where we find the basis of the pope's authority in the Catholic Church, since the successors of St. Peter sit in the Chair of Peter in Rome. The center of Matthew's Gospel is the Sermon on the Mount. This is the parable where Jesus teaches us how to live the Kingdom of God. During this year, we will hear an extensive reading of six weeks, starting from the fourth Sunday in ordinary time to the ninth Sunday in ordinary time.

At the start of Advent, Matthew focuses on Christ's promised second coming at the end of time. St. John the Baptist holds a prominent place in the gospel during the second and third Sunday of the season. John the Baptist is really the forerunner for Christ. His mission is to testify of the importance of repenting and preparing for the Kingdom of God. Once we reach the fourth Sunday of Advent, the Blessed Virgin Mary is the central figure of the gospel. This is the gospel where we hear she is with child and of her betrothal to St. Joseph.

The liturgical year, Cycle B, will highlight the gospel of Mark. Throughout Mark's Gospel we experience theological insights about Christian life in Christ. Mark has created for us a brilliant theological narrative that is relevant for us today as it was when it was originally written. The evangelist teaches that our baptism unites us all to Christ and joins us together at the Eucharistic meal to experience new life with God.

The Gospel of Luke is highlighted in Year C of the liturgical year. All four Sundays proclaim a Lucan passage and begin in a reverse time frame scenario. We will hear on the first Sunday of Advent the signs that will inaugurate Christ's second coming. John the Baptist is the focus of the Gospel on the second and third Sundays of Advent. John is the precursor who inaugurated the adult ministry of Jesus, by announcing that God's Kingdom is near and calling people to conversion and a change of heart. The fourth Sunday of Advent presents Mary and Elizabeth, the two pregnant women who cooperated with

God's plan and who will be instrumental in helping to bring about God's reign and salvation to all people.

The Blessed Virgin Mary also holds a prominent place on December 8, which is the Solemnity of the Immaculate Conception of the Blessed Virgin Mary. It is the Patronal Feast Day of the United States and a holyday of obligation. This solemnity praises God for Mary's total freedom from original sin from the moment of her conception. Mary under the title of Our Lady of Guadalupe is celebrated on December 12. We are reminded during this feast of Mary's motherly care not only for our Hispanic brothers and sisters but also for all people of America.

During the holy season of Advent, the weekday Lectionary is really separated into two distinct sections; the first from the beginning of Advent through December 16 and the second from December 17 through December 24, known as late Advent. The beginning section has passages from the prophet Isaiah. In the second part of the season, the readings lead us from the birth of St. John the Baptist to the birth of Christ.

Advent's final days provide us an excellent opportunity to reflect on the various titles the Old Testament writers gave to the longed for Messiah. We call these titles the O Antiphons: O Adonai, O Root of Jesse, O Key of David, O Rising Sun, O King of Nations, O Emmanuel. An interesting feature of these antiphons is that in Latin, and ordered from last to first, the initial letters of the seven antiphons form an acrostic that spells the Latin words *ero cras*, which means, "Tomorrow I will come." When we sing the hymn "O Come, O Come, Emmanuel" you will hear the O Antiphons throughout the piece. We pray these "O" Antiphons at vespers starting on December 17.

Advent is all about waiting to receive the light of Christ into our world. It is a time of new beginnings. We watch, prepare, make straight the path, and we trust and believe. May this Advent be a prayerful time for you as you await the coming of our Savior. Peace!

CHRISTMAS

Christmas is one of the most important days of the church year, second only to Easter itself. It is the feast of the incarnation, the feast of God becoming flesh. At Christmas, the Divine becomes one of us. Jesus is Emmanuel (God with us). Every time we celebrate the holy sacrifice of the Mass, the bread and wine are transformed into his Body and Blood, so in a sense, the feast of the incarnation occurs over and over again.

Celebrating Christmas is more than one day. "The liturgical season of Christmas begins with Evening Prayer of the Nativity of the Lord up to and including the Sunday after Epiphany or after January 6" (Universal Norms on the Liturgical Year, #33). An easy way to remember this is the liturgical season of Christmas time begins with the Vigil Mass on Christmas Eve and concludes on the Feast of the Baptism of the Lord. During this season, we celebrate the birth of Christ into our world and into our hearts.

There are four different prayer texts associated with December 24 and 25. Each Mass has its own set of prayers to correspond with the time of the celebration. Each of these prayer texts has an abundance of theology associate with them. The Vigil Mass is the first Mass celebrated on Christmas Eve. The prayer text speaks about the anticipation we have for welcoming our redeemer, "As we look forward, O Lord, to the coming festivities, may we serve you all the more eagerly" (Roman Missal, Christmas Vigil Mass, Prayer Over the Offerings). The prayers for the Mass during the night, originally called the Midnight Mass, reminds us of the importance of this sacred night, "O God, who have made this most sacred night radiant with the splendor of the true light" (Roman Missal, At the Mass during the Night, Collect). This symbol of light coming into the world continues in the prayers from The Mass at Dawn. The priest prays, "Grant, we pray, Almighty God, that, as we are bathed in the new radiance of your incarnate Word, the light of faith, which illumines our minds, may also shine through our deeds" (Roman Missal, At the Mass at Dawn, Collect). When the celebrant prays from the Mass during the day, we hear of the connection between the divinity of Christ and the dignity of humanity. "O God, who wonderfully created the dignity of human nature and still more wonderfully restored it, grant, we pray, that we may share in the divinity of Christ who humbled himself to share in our humanity" (Roman Missal, At the Mass during the Day, Collect). It is interesting to note that the last half of this prayer (from the grant, we pray) is always said quietly when the priest or deacon pours a little water into the chalice filled with wine during the Liturgy of the Eucharist. Over the course of these four Masses we experience the Nativity of the Lord, the Son of God and Son of Mary. Reflecting on these prayers reminds us to proclaim this Good News to all we encounter.

The Roman Missal includes three Prefaces (the prayer before the Holy, Holy, Holy) that can be prayed on the Solemnity of Christmas, and throughout the entire liturgical season, each one containing its own theme and theology. Preface I speaks of Christ as a new light of God's holy glory, "For in the mystery of the Word made flesh a new light of your glory has shone upon the eyes of our mind" (Roman Missal, Preface I Nativity of the Lord). Preface II tells of the incarnation restoring all things, "Raising up in himself all that was cast down, he might restore unity to all creation and call straying humanity back to the heavenly Kingdom" (Roman Missal, Preface II Nativity of the Lord). Preface III reminds us of the holy exchange that restores our life, "For through him the holy exchange that restores our life has shone forth today in splendor" (Roman Missal, Preface III Nativity of the Lord).

The liturgical color for the Christmas season is white. In addition to the traditional crèche, the worship space may include poinsettias, wreaths, trees, greenery, and lighting. All the greenery should be real rather than artificial. This follows the guidance from the liturgical document entitled "Built of Living Stones Art, Architecture, and Worship" (BLS). The bishops teach us in this document, "The use of living flowers and plants, rather than artificial greens, serves as a reminder of the gift of life God has given to the human community" (BLS, #129).

In its present form the custom of displaying figures depicting the birth of Jesus Christ owes its origin to St. Francis of Assisi who made the Christmas crèche or manger for Christmas Eve of 1223. When a manger scene is set up in the home, it is appropriate that it should be blest. Here is the blessing of a manger or nativity scene from *The Book of Blessings*:

> God of every nation and people, from the very beginning of creation you have made manifest your love: when our need for a Savior was great you sent your Son to be born of the Virgin Mary. To our lives he brings joy and peace, justice, mercy, and love.
>
> Lord, bless all who look upon this manger; may it remind us of the humble birth of Jesus, and raise up our thoughts to him, who is God-with-us and Savior of all, and who lives and reigns for ever and ever. Amen.

WINTER ORDINARY TIME

Between the Feast of the Baptism of the Lord and Ash Wednesday, liturgically we return to ordinary time. Now that the Christmas season is over, we seem to go back to a normal schedule for school, work, and family life. To the start of Lent is a full eight weeks, as we celebrate with seven Sundays of ordinary time.

We must remember ordinary time does not mean "not special" or truly ordinary, for all time is important. When we speak about ordinary time liturgically, we really mean the counting of the weeks, as in ordinal numbering (i.e., second, third, fourth, fifth, etc.). During this time, we celebrate the mystery of Christ (Universal Norms on the Liturgical Year, #43). During the second through the eighth Sunday of ordinary time, we have the opportunity to reflect on what it means to be a follower of Christ.

This reflection also includes what accepting that call really means for us as Christians. During winter ordinary time, the meaning of discipleship really comes down to our willingness to travel with Jesus, through Sacred Scripture, just as the first disciples did when he healed the sick, fed the hungry, cast out demons, and ate with sinners and tax collectors. The church offers us this liturgical time so we can pause to consider what God is doing in us, with Jesus and through our relationship with Christ and the Holy Spirit. We are disciples of Christ, and that relationship has responsibilities. Liturgical composer and clinician Tom Kenzia teaches, "We are called to be the hands and feet, eyes and ears of Christ, ready to serve our brothers and sisters in need as He would do" (*Clothed in Love*).

When we are in Year A of the Sunday Lectionary, the Old Testament readings explore the covenant between God and the Israelites. Throughout these readings, the Israelites are assured of God's promise to watch over them and protect them. The covenant though is not one sided, it has responsibilities for the people themselves. St Paul's First Letter to the Corinthians comprises the New Testament readings. It is here where Paul established his own mission rooted in Jesus name.

The predominate gospel texts are from St. Matthew. Chapter 5 of the evangelist is proclaimed from the fourth Sunday to the seventh Sunday of ordinary time. This chapter is the section concerning the Sermon on the Mount, which begins with Jesus's teaching in the Beatitudes. These Beatitudes teach us that we can rejoice and be glad as disciples of Christ because he will never forget us and our discipleship will lead us to the Kingdom of Heaven.

The inspiration on discipleship occurs in Year B of the liturgical cycle. During the Sunday readings during the Liturgy of the Word, the first readings will be taken from a variety of Old Testament books. We will hear the call of Samuel, then a passage from the prophet Jonah, which tells us about Nineveh's change of heart and then God's merciful response. We get to hear the words of Moses to the people telling them the Lord will raise up a prophet who will speak God's words. From the book of Job, we hear about all his life's drudgery and how Job never loses faith. On the sixth Sunday of ordinary time we hear the passage from Leviticus that tells us how a person with leprosy was considered unclean and an outsider to the community until they were cleaned ritually.

All these Old Testament readings are paired with gospel passages that help us reflect on the concept of discipleship and what it means to be a disciple. On the second week of ordinary time, we hear the call of the first disciples. We hear St. Mark's gospel passage that teaches us the initial step in discipleship is repentance, which is really turning one's heart away from evil and toward God. When we hear the gospel from the fourth Sunday in ordinary time, we experience Jesus as the fulfillment of Moses's words. In the gospel, the words of Jesus actually expel unclean spirits. Throughout this time, we hear about the faith of many people and the many miracles Jesus performs because of this faith. The Lord's compassion shines, and his ministry constantly grows in leaps and bounds.

The Sunday gospel readings during this time in Year C of the Lectionary teach us about the start of the public ministry of Jesus. We hear from the evangelist St. Luke, about his first public miracle at the Wedding Feast of Cana and also the calling of the original disciples. These same themes are echoed in the first readings each Sunday. We will hear the last third of St. Paul's Letter to the Corinthians as the content of the second reading during this liturgical season. This last section of St. Paul's letter will focus on the Christian community and the bonds which actually united them to each other. The main themes during this section of the letter will include the Spirit, love, and faith in the message of the Gospel.

These themes of missionary discipleship, which are part of the Liturgy of the Word during winter ordinary time, fit right into the Apostolic Exhortation *Evangelii guadium (The Joy of the Gospel),* written by Pope Francis. The pope teaches, "Each Christian and every community must discern the path that the Lord points out, but all of us are asked to obey his call to go forth from our own comfort zone in order to reach all the "peripheries" in need of the light of the Gospel" (*Evangelii guadium* EG, #20). These "peripheries" of which the pope writes about are actually our own social, family, and work environments. In other words, we are called to proclaim the Gospel whenever we come in contact with people. We truly are called to be missionary disciples.

As we move from the white vestments of the Christmas season to the green vestments of ordinary time, our liturgical environment also changes. The red and white poinsettias give way to green flowered plants. The liturgical color is green, yet nature provides us with beautiful accents of winter. During the darkness of winter, the church as well as nature increases the light as we celebrate the Feast of the Presentation of the Lord. This feast, which is also called Candlemas Day, is celebrated on February 2. On this day, we bless the candles that will be used for all our liturgies throughout the year. The next day, February 3, some of these same candles will be used to bless throats as we celebrate the Optional Memorial of St. Blaise, the bishop and martyr. During this time, our liturgical calendar has many other days that call us to remember those holy men and women who have lived the faith and are in their heavenly home.

The readings for this liturgical time help us to become better people, better disciples for the Lord. God continues to call us in our time and in our own situations. May these weeks of winter ordinary time help us to see how God is present in our lives today. May we be open to the power of the Holy Spirit to realize the opportunities given to us to serve those in need.

LENT—A LITURGICAL OVERVIEW

Lent begins each year on Ash Wednesday with the blessing and distribution of ashes and concludes on Holy Thursday before the evening Mass of the Lord's Supper. In order to give the church a renewed sense of Lent, the Second Vatican Council set forth the liturgical agenda: "Lent is marked by two themes, the baptismal and the penitential" *(Constitution on the Sacred Liturgy, #109).*

Two celebrations mark the beginning of Lent and include the entire worshipping community but especially those participating in the Rite of Christian Initiation of Adults (RCIA). The two celebrations are the Rite of Sending at the parish and the Rite of Election, which is at the cathedral. In addition, the Scrutinies are celebrated on the third, fourth, and fifth Sundays of Lent. These rites confer strength on the elect and confront all the faithful present with the need for conversion. The elects are present at the Liturgy of the Word, as living icons of the season's baptismal character, the principal symbols of Lent.

The prescribed liturgical color for Lent is violet. The vestments worn by the priest and deacon will be a different shade of violet compared to that of Advent since we are celebrating a different liturgical aspect of the Paschal Mystery (the life, death, and resurrection of Jesus). The Lenten shade is a darker violet than the lighter shade for Advent.

The Lenten texts for the liturgy of the Word inspire us to repent and believe in the gospel. During the holy season of Lent, our entire church truly goes on a spiritual retreat. The Sacred Scripture proclaimed during this season gives us guidance for our spiritual journey. We are called to have a change of heart. This metanoia (which means change in one's way of life resulting from penitence or spiritual conversion) is actually an ongoing process, which includes our attitudes and actions. Throughout this liturgical season, the lectionary offers us the opportunity to hear of God's mercy, love, forgiveness, and guidance. This rich Lenten banquet is an excellent source for our soul searching and change of heart.

The Sunday readings in the Year A cycle of the lectionary are dominated by the three great narratives found in St. John's account of the Gospel: Jesus meeting and talking with the Samaritan woman at the well; the healing of the man born blind; and the raising of Lazarus. These texts are so important that they are always proclaimed on the third, fourth, and fifth Sundays of Lent during the scrutiny masses even when we are in Cycles B and C of the lectionary. The first Sunday of Lent always includes the gospel about the temptation of Jesus in the wilderness, followed by the Transfiguration of Jesus in the presence of Peter, James, and John during the second Sunday of Lent.

The seasonal Psalm of Lent is Psalm 51, also known as the miserere, which is first proclaimed on Ash Wednesday. This sacred text, prayed by Jesus himself, helps us understand the main focus of the season: "A clean heart create for me, O God, and a steadfast spirit renew within me." This refrain teaches us that it is actually God who brings about our conversion. Our participation in this metanoia is to place ourselves in his presence. This same Psalm is also recited every Friday morning as part of Morning Prayer or Lauds.

Each week the Presider Prayers integrate the images, themes, and theology of the gospel text; so in the proclamation of the Gospels the whole community, especially the elect, come to a deeper understanding of who Christ is and what he can do in our lives. These Gospels proclaim to all of us that Christ is truly our Savior and Redeemer.

Prayer, fasting, and almsgiving are the traditional disciplines of the observance of Lent. The Stations of the Cross is a time-honored tradition, which we pray each week in church. Lent is also a perfect time for *Lectio divina,* "holy reading," a custom embraced by many as an oasis of peace in this busy world.

The Triduum, which stands at the heart of the Paschal cycle, includes Holy Thursday, Good Friday, and Holy Saturday. These three days are an intense immersion in the fundamental mystery of what it is to be a Christian and to be Church. Let us plan now to attend and actively participate in the Holy Thursday, Good Friday, and Holy Saturday celebrations. Lent (the forty days), the Paschal Triduum (the three days), and Easter time (the fifty days) are truly opportunities to live our faith and encounter our Lord.

Pope Francis in his Apostolic Exhortation *Evangelii gaudium* (The *Joy of the Gospel)* speaks to all of us about the challenges we face as we attempt to live our faith. During this Lenten time of introspection, may our prayer, fasting, and almsgiving help us to reflect on the Cross of Christ so we may become a better disciple of the Lord.

HOLY WEEK

The celebrations of Holy Week help us to focus on the fact that "the days of his saving Passion and glorious Resurrection are approaching" (*Preface II of the Passion of the Lord, Roman Missal*). Here is a brief overview of the many celebrations that occur during Holy Week:

Holy Week begins with the celebration of Palm Sunday of the Passion of the Lord. Palm branches are ancient symbols of hope, victory, and new life, so they are a part of our Palm Sunday celebration. The gospel proclaimed on Palm Sunday celebrates the Lord's triumphant entrance into Jerusalem where he was welcomed by crowds worshiping him and laying down palm leaves before him. Together we too will carry palm branches and join in the proclamation of the gospel.

The Chrism Mass is celebrated at the cathedral during Holy Week. During this Mass, the holy oils that will be used throughout the coming year are blessed by the bishop. All the priests of the diocese also renew publicly their priestly promises.

In many churches, the Tenebrae service is celebrated in the evening. The term Tenebrae means "darkness" in Latin. It refers to the public praying of the liturgy of the Hours. It consists of prayers, readings, music, and candles that will be extinguished throughout the service.

The summit of the liturgical year is the Easter Triduum—from the evening of Holy Thursday to the evening of Easter Sunday. Though chronologically three days, they are liturgically one day unfolding for us the unity of Christ's Paschal Mystery (Jesus's life, death, and resurrection). The single celebration of the Triduum marks the end of the Lenten season and leads to the Mass of the resurrection of the Lord at the Easter Vigil. The liturgical services that take place during the Triduum are the Mass of the Lord's Supper,

Good Friday of the Lord's Passion, and the Mass of the Resurrection of the Lord.

The Mass of the Lord's Supper (Holy Thursday) commemorates the institution of Eucharist and the priesthood, as well as Jesus's command to love and serve one another. During this Mass, the celebrant will receive the holy oils that were blessed by the bishop. The connection between the Eucharist and living a life of service is ritualized by the Washing of Feet. The *Ceremonial of Bishops* (CB) sets the context in no. 297: "This Mass is, first of all, the memorial of the institution of the Eucharist. It is also the memorial of the institution of the priesthood, by which Christ's mission and sacrifice are perpetuated in the world. In addition, this Mass is the memorial of that love by which the Lord loved us even to death" (CB, #297).

During this Mass of the Lord's Supper, the celebrant will consecrate enough hosts for this Mass and also enough for the following day's celebration, since the Passion of the Lord is the only day in the liturgical year where a Mass is not to be celebrated.

Following Communion, the transfer of the Blessed Sacrament begins with a procession to the chapel. All present are part of this procession as we prepare to spend a period of time with the Lord in adoration until twelve midnight. There is no formal or specific dismissal to the Mass on this night, emphasizing that the liturgies of the Sacred Paschal Triduum are actually one continuous liturgy that spans over three days.

On Good Friday (Friday of the Passion of the Lord) we gather together to prayerfully recall the death of Jesus. Just as the Holy Thursday Liturgy had no formal ending, the Good Friday service has no formal beginning, offering us a unity between both celebrations. The service includes the proclamation of the Passion, the adoration of the holy cross, and a Communion service.

When the service does begin, it happens with the clergy prostrating themselves on the floor of the sanctuary while the rest of the assembly kneels. It is very striking with a noticeable silence to help us remember what we are celebrating.

The Liturgy of the Word takes place with the proclamation of the Lord's Passion. Following the homily, the solemn intercessions are proclaimed. These ten intercessions reveal the universality of our prayer, showing how important it is for the church to spend an abundance of time pleading for the well-being of the entire world.

The next part of the Good Friday service is the adoration of the holy cross. The Church provides us the opportunity to show our sign of reverence to the cross with a simple genuflection, a kiss, a touch of the wood of the cross, or a bow toward the cross. When adoration is finished, the distribution of Holy Communion begins.

The liturgy ends as simply as it began. There is a brief dismissal, but no procession, giving everyone an opportunity to continue adoring the cross for as long as desired.

Celebrating the liturgies of Holy Week allows us to experience through powerful rituals the same experiences Jesus and his disciples walked on their profound journey.

Holy Saturday morning is a time for the Church to wait at the Lord's tomb as we pray, fast, and mediate on his Passion and Death as we await his Resurrection. We celebrate Morning Prayer with the elect as they continue preparing for the Easter sacraments. We do not celebrate Mass during the day.

The climax of the Sacred Paschal Triduum, the Easter Vigil, begins after darkness has fallen. St. Augustine calls the Easter Vigil "the mother of all vigils." The Universal Norms on the Liturgical Year (UNLY) teaches, "The Sacred Paschal Triduum of the Passion and Resurrection of the Lord shines forth as the high point of the entire liturgical year" (UNLY, #18). The Triduum ranks highest among the celebrations of the liturgical year.

The four parts of the Easter Vigil take us through a gradual unfolding of the Paschal Mystery of Christ. The first part is the solemn beginning of the vigil or Lucernarium. Outside on the plaza, we stand by the blazing fire for the blessing on the fire and the preparation of the candle. This is followed by the Liturgy of the Word, which reminds us how God is revealing to us his plan for salvation history. Next is the baptismal liturgy, which draws the elect through the waters of baptism into the promise of eternal life. We the faithful also renew our own baptismal promises. The newly baptized and those who are making a profession of faith will also celebrate the sacrament of Confirmation. The Liturgy of the Eucharist is the climax of the Easter Vigil celebration. The newly initiated join for the first time with the faithful the receiving of the Lord's Body and Blood. Together we experience the presence of the Risen Lord within our midst.

On Easter Sunday, we renew our baptismal promises and are sprinkled with Holy Water to once again renew and refresh us. Pope Francis in *Evangelii gaudium* (EG) calls us to be an Alleluia people who evangelize with joy and connect our liturgy with our life. The Holy Father teaches, "Evangelization with joy becomes beauty in the liturgy, as part of our daily concern to spread goodness" (EG, #24).

Celebrating each of these liturgies gives us an opportunity to enter into the mystery and presence of God each day as we experience the life, death, and resurrection of Jesus.

THE EASTER SEASON

Jesus Christ is risen today, Alleluia!

Easter Sunday is the greatest of all Sundays, and Easter time is the most important of all liturgical times. Our Easter joy and celebration continues for fifty days as we reflect on the richness of our Lord's Passion, Death, Resurrection, Ascension, and Glorification. The season ends with the sending of the Holy Spirit at Pentecost. The Universal Norms on the Liturgical Year and the General Roman Calendar teach us, "The fifty days from Easter Sunday to Pentecost are celebrated in joyful exaltation as one feast, or better, as one 'great Sunday'" (UNLY, #22).

Fifty days are a seventh of the year, and so we keep our fifty-day Easter time as a long Lord's Day, the "great Sunday." Fifty days are a week of weeks plus a day, a symbol of eternity. And so we keep Easter time living as if God's reign has already come. Christians, newly baptized and long baptized, are to live in the wedding feast of heaven and earth, no fasting, no mourning, endlessly singing our Alleluia.

Easter time is not just remembering something that happened long ago. It is Christ dead and risen in our midst. It is the Spirit breathing in us today. Easter is made present in the neophytes, the newly baptized among us. We bless ourselves in church with the water blest at the font during the great Easter Vigil, and we renew our baptismal promises once again. We continue to smell the sweet fragrance of the Sacred Chrism used to anoint those who received Confirmation at the mother of all vigils, and we are nourished by the Body and Blood of our Risen Lord in the Eucharist.

The word "Easter" comes from Old English, meaning simply the "East." The sun, which rises in the East, bringing light, warmth, and hope, is a symbol for the Christian of the rising Christ, who is the true Light of the world. The paschal candle is a central symbol of this divine light, which is Christ. It is placed at the ambo before the singing of the Exsultet (The Easter Proclamation) at the Easter Vigil. It is the *light of Christ, rising in glory*, scattering the darkness of our hearts and minds. It is kept near the ambo throughout Easter time and lit for all liturgical celebrations. Normally the paschal candle is lit at Baptisms and funerals and the newly baptized actually receive their baptismal candles lit from the paschal candle. The Church is very clear on the specifics of this important symbol. This candle should be made of wax, never be artificial, be replaced each year, be only one in number, and be of sufficiently large size that it may convey the truth that Christ is the light of the world.

The parish liturgical environment can contains lilies and flowering, colorful, fragrant plants, which are all signs of new life. The liturgical color for the season is white, with red vestments appearing when we celebrate Pentecost.

Easter time marks the beginning of the period of mystagogia for the neophytes. During this time, they reflect on the meaning of the Sacred Scriptures, the celebration of the sacraments, and their new life in Christ. This joyful season is also a time for us to reflect on our life in the Church. One way to accomplish this is to meditate on and follow the events told to us in the Gospels of the season. These fifty days are highlighted by the Risen Lord's appearances, the proclamation of the disciples concerning the resurrection of Jesus, the healing of the sick, all the baptizing that occurred, the ascending of Jesus to the Father, and the disciples receiving the Holy Spirit.

The lectionary readings for the first eight days of Easter, called the Octave of Easter, highlight the start and growth of the communities after Pentecost, while proclaiming the living presence of Jesus. Throughout the Easter season, the readings from the Acts of the Apostles highlight many of the people, especially Peter and Paul, who played significant roles in the preaching of the Word to others. As the people of God, we hike the road of Emmaus and picnic by the Sea of Galilee and climb the Mount of Olives.

One of the theological themes of Easter is from death to new life. Here in our hemisphere we experience the season of springtime, which also helps us to appreciate all the new life we see around us.

The grass grows, flowers bloom, and the trees continue to bud. In our church, the liturgy really uses these same elements from God's created world as we gather to praise and thank God for all he has done for us. Throughout our liturgical celebrations, we get to us all of our senses. We see and touch water, smell and see flowers, see the light of the paschal candle, hear and sing beautiful music, and taste the wheat and wine when we consume Jesus in the consecrated host and wine.

The church asks us to celebrate Easter for fifty days because the Easter mysteries have so much for us to reflect upon, appreciate, and absorb into our daily lives.

SUMMER ORDINARY TIME

After being placed on hold by the great ninety days of Lent, the Sacred Paschal Triduum and Easter time, the church once again resumes ordinary time on the liturgical calendar. Ordinary time refers to "counted time" or "ordered time" (coming from the Latin root *ordanalis*). This time is ordered or counted around the Paschal Mystery of Christ.

Liturgists speak of summer ordinary time as the calendar time from after the celebration of Pentecost to September. The Universal Norms on the Liturgical Year and the Calendar (UNLY) teach us, "Besides the times of the year that have their own distinctive character, there remain in the yearly cycle thirty-three or thirty-four weeks in which no particular aspect of the mystery of Christ is celebrated, but rather the mystery of Christ itself is honored in its fullness, especially on the Sundays. This period is known as Ordinary Time" (UNLY, #43).

While ordinary may suggest something usual, this liturgical time is very significant for our growth in faith. It is during this part of the liturgical year that we have the opportunity to integrate those experiences we encountered from Lent to Pentecost. There is nothing ordinary about people of faith who gather each Sunday to become who we are destined to be by virtue of our Baptism—the Body of Christ. Sunday is the original feast day.

The Universal Norms on the Liturgical Year and the Calendar instruct us, "On the first day of each week, which is known as the Day of the Lord or the Lord's Day, the Church by an apostolic tradition that draws its origin from the very day of the resurrection of Christ, celebrates the Paschal Mystery (the life, death, and resurrection of Christ). Hence, Sunday must be considered the primordial feast day" (UNLY, #4).

As we resume Ordinary Time on the day after Pentecost, we begin with the week that allows the church cycle to end after the thirty-fourth Sunday, better known as the Solemnity of Our Lord Jesus Christ, King of the Universe. Since Easter is a moveable feast, many years we will jump ahead liturgically.

The liturgical color for ordinary time is green, a symbol of new growth and life in the Church, yet our Sunday liturgical color will not change to green until after the solemnities of the Most Holy Trinity and the Most Holy Body and Blood of Christ. Since it is summertime, our liturgical environment will have a variety of fresh flowers and reflects the cycle of nature throughout our worship space.

When Year A is designated for the liturgical year, the Sunday Lectionary Gospel readings continue from St. Matthew (after the two above mentioned solemnities). In the Sunday gospels proclaimed in July, we hear the parables concerning the building of the kingdom through the stories of the sower and the seed, and the weeds and the wheat. The language and the imagery of the parables functions like a veil, since it both reveals and conceals meaning. It is not enough just to hear the Word of God, we are called to also be open to it and accept it. When we avail ourselves to God's Word and seek to understand it, God opens our minds and hearts to give us his wisdom and keeps us on his right path. We hear this expressed in the Collect (the Opening Prayer of Mass) of the fifteenth Sunday in ordinary time, when the celebrant prays, "O God, who show the light of your truth to those who go astray, so that they may return to the right path, give all who for the faith they profess are accounted Christians the grace to reject whatever is contrary to the name of Christ and to strive after all that does it honor" (Roman Missal, third edition).

During summer ordinary time in Cycle B, we hear from the Gospel of Mark during the tenth Sunday through the sixteenth Sunday of the liturgical year. During the following five Sundays starting on the seventeenth Sunday in ordinary time and continuing through to the twenty-first Sunday, have the opportunity to proclaim scripture passages from the Gospel of John, known as the Bread of Life discourse. These famous selections remind us that Jesus is truly the Bread of Life, the Living Bread that has come down from heaven. Starting on the twenty-second Sunday, we return to the gospel of Mark and hear familiar themes. These include the importance of taking up one's cross, the disciples wanting to following Jesus, even though he is predicting is own Passion, Death, and Resurrection, and the need to love God and others as a way to inherit the Kingdom of Heaven. If this were not tough enough, Jesus teaches the need to sell all possessions

When we are in Year C of the Sunday Lectionary, the gospel readings continue from St. Luke. Throughout this time, the theme of discipleship is prominent. In Luke, the disciples are called to identify with the mind and spirit of Jesus who is totally concerned with the poor, the outcast, the elderly, the afflicted, and the sinner. The disciples are called to embrace these same concerns. This has implications for all of us. As disciples of Christ we too are challenged to be open, welcoming, and forgiving as Christ is to others especially to the poor and the oppressed. The preaching and ministry of Jesus emphasizes that his followers are to be aware of their need to pray in order to accomplish the ministry in which they were called. Jesus asks us to serve others out of a true sense of self-giving and sacrifice.

We are called to share God's holy Word in both word and action, this joy of the Gospel every day and in all situations. Pope Francis reminds us, "Our workplaces are critical locations in which we can become the leaven of God's kingdom" (*Evangelii guadium,* #75).

Summer ordinary time is not a time to take off from one's faith journey; rather it's a time to relax while appreciating all of God's beautiful creation. In the Sunday lectionary readings, during this liturgical time in Matthews's account of the gospel, we are taught that to be a disciple of the Jesus we must take up our cross and follow him. Through the use of parables, the Son of God instructs the disciples (and us) about what it really means to serve Jesus. Throughout Sacred Scripture Jesus gives us a glimpse, sometimes more clearly than others, that he must suffer and die.

This is the time where we can have more one-on-one time with Jesus as we enjoy the beauty of the summer months. As life slows down, be sure to spend time in prayer. Allow God the opportunity to speak to you so you can share your joys and blessings with others. Ordinary time is not ordinary at all; rather it is very significant for our growth in faith!

Fall Ordinary Time

Ordinary time refers to "counted time" or "ordered time" (coming from the Latin root *ordanalis*). This time is ordered or counted around the Paschal Mystery of Christ. Liturgists speak of fall ordinary time as the calendar time from September to Advent. The Universal Norms on the Liturgical Year and the Calendar (UNLY) teach us, "Besides the times of the year that have their own distinctive character, there remain in the yearly cycle thirty-three or thirty-four weeks in which no particular aspect of the mystery of Christ is celebrated, but rather the mystery of Christ itself is honored in its fullness, especially on the Sundays. This period is known as Ordinary Time" (UNLY, #43).

This portion of ordinary time bridges a change in season in the natural world from summer to autumn, while we celebrate all aspects of the mystery of Christ. In autumn, the world of nature is preparing us for winter. This season is really a process. Daylight decreases gradually, leaves turn and eventually fall from trees, and there is a change in the weather. These turning leaves are reminders of our mortality and also the beauty of creation.

During ordinary time the church invites us to discover connections between the events of our own lives and God's Word revealed in sacred Scripture and celebrated in the liturgy. The lectionary offers a wide variety of themes, teachings, and episodes in the life of Jesus for us to mediate. Through Sacred Scripture we learn more about the life of Jesus and the early Church.

In Cycle "A" of the Sunday liturgical readings we hear what it takes, according to St. Matthew, to be a disciple of Jesus. It is plain and simple, but not necessarily easy. We are told that to be a disciple we must take up our cross and follow the master. If that were not enough, we hear later in that same gospel, how Jesus teaches his disciples about forgiveness. Jesus continues to use parables to instruct his disciples and all of us. Throughout this fall ordinary time, our Lord speaks about how he will suffer and die, which confuses St. Peter. As we get closer to the end of the liturgical year in this lectionary cycle, we hear how the Pharisees try to trick Jesus about paying taxes to Caesar. All this is leading up to Jesus pointing out what it takes to inherit the kingdom of heaven.

We focus on the Gospel of Mark in lectionary Cycle B. As we read the gospel text during fall ordinary time, we will see a pattern in Jesus's teaching method that will be repeated in the weeks ahead. Jesus's first teaching is directed to the Pharisees who questioned him. His words are then addressed to the crowd, and then finally to his disciples, who in turn questioned him about what he had taught. Mark's narrative shows several audiences for Jesus's teaching: his antagonists, the crowds, and Jesus's disciples. The words to the Pharisees are sometimes words filled with challenge. The teachings Jesus shares with the crowds is of a more general in subject matter. When the Master talks to the disciples, they usually misunderstand him, so Jesus must give them a further explanation about the message he presented and its associated meaning.

Throughout this portion of the Gospel, we hear many themes: the importance of taking up one's cross daily and follow Christ as he predicts his own Passion, Death, and Resurrection; Jesus speaking about inheriting the Kingdom of God; the Kingdom of God which is both here now, but will only be fully realized when we reach our heavenly home; the importance of loving God and all those around us; and the giving away of all the possessions one has earned.

In the last three months of ordinary time, the Gospel of St Luke, in Cycle C of the lectionary, provides us with an abundance of themes through parables for us to contemplate. We will hear three parables about the unending love of God the Father: the lost sheep, the lost coin, and the prodigal son. The evangelist gives us the opportunity to reflect on stewardship and the importance of wisely using the gifts that have been bestowed on each one of us. Discipleship also is presented to us through the parable of the rich man and Lazarus. Many of the stories we hear throughout this liturgical season show us the teaching of Jesus that deal with care for the poor, the outcast, and all those in need of compassion.

As we journey in faith, we observe a variety of solemnities and feasts throughout this season and we learn more about many saints and our Catholic tradition. Throughout this time, we celebrate the feasts of the Nativity of the Blessed Virgin Mary, the Exaltation of the Holy Cross, the Archangels (Michael, Gabriel, and Raphael), the evangelists St. Matthew and St. Luke, and Saints Simon and Jude, two of the apostles.

On November 18, we celebrate the Dedication of the Lateran Basilica, which is one of the four major basilicas in Rome. The Lateran Basilica is actually the cathedral church of the Pope (not St. Peter's Basilica). During this time, we also celebrate the memorials of St. Charles Borromeo, a bishop who did much concerning liturgical renewal around the time of the Council of Trent and St. Cecilia, the patron of pastoral musicians.

In addition to this small sample of feast days, this liturgical time also includes the Solemnity of All Saints Day on November 1. This day gives us an opportunity to remember all the known and unknown saints who have entered the heavenly kingdom. The Commemoration of All the Faithful Departed (All Souls' Day) on November 2 helps us remember all who have "gone before us with the sign of faith and rest in the sleep of peace" (Roman Missal, Eucharistic Prayer 1).

At the end of November, we celebrate the Solemnity of Our Lord Jesus Christ, King of the Universe. This solemnity goes back to 1925, when Pope Pius XI added it to the liturgical calendar. As we celebrate this solemnity, we are reminded that "Our Lord Jesus Christ was anointed with the oil of gladness as the eternal Priest and King of all creation" (Roman Missal, Preface: Christ, King of the Universe).

The liturgical color is green, yet nature provides us with beautiful accents, so you will see the colors of fall throughout the liturgical space. The mums that are starting to appear in the liturgical environment show us colors associated with the harvest season. The liturgical environment committee should prepare the worship space to correspond with the readings of this section of ordinary time, which focus more attention to the "last things" of fall, especially as we enter the month of November.

We pray in the Preface for Sundays in Ordinary Time V, "You laid the foundations of the world and have arranged the changing of times and seasons" (Roman Missal). Jesus made great use of the cycle of nature in his teachings and parables. The natural seasons provided the backdrop against which Jesus could speak of faith, the need to believe, and of God's reign.

Fall ordinary time helps us to celebrate many aspects of the Paschal Mystery of Christ throughout all of creation, and in our personal and liturgical life.

Liturgical Rites

According to the teaching of the Second Vatican Council, care must be taken to ensure that the rites are marked by a noble simplicity. The beauty of the Roman Catholic liturgy lies in its ability for all the faithful to understand the meaning and movement of the liturgy so they can participate with full, conscious and active participation. (*Ceremonial of Bishops: Chapter 4, no. 55)*

THE COLLEGE OF CARDINALS

The College of Cardinals is the select group of bishops whose primary function is electing a new pope following the death or resignation of the previous one. Their secondary responsibility is to serve as a body of advisors to the Holy Father. The number of times the college is convened depends upon each individual pope. More contemporary and recent popes such as St. John Paul II and Pope Francis have increasingly sought their council.

The title of cardinal is largely honorific. Traditionally, the word *cardinal* has been translated from the Latin *cardo* or in English as *hinge*, signifying connecting the pope with the rest of the world. The Holy Father often appoints cardinals as members of Vatican committees and sometimes designates them to serve as his official representative for an event when he cannot personally be present.

The earliest cardinals were priests of Rome thus they had a strong connection to Rome. As the Church grew, it became increasingly evident that the College of Cardinals needed to represent the entire Church, not just that of in Rome.

New cardinals make an oath of obedience to the Holy Father at their elevation. In it they acknowledge they have now "become members of the Roman clergy." Eventually the practice arose of assigning each cardinal to a particular church in the city of Rome—their titular church. "The Cardinals are not involved in the daily administration or sacramental duties of their titular church, but when in Rome, they will celebrate Mass there, and often provide financial support to maintain their titular churches" (Code of Canon Law, #357).

The selection of new members of the College of Cardinals is left solely to the current pope. Traditionally, in the past, those chosen were the heads of the major offices of the Vatican and those who were diocesan bishops from around the world. More recent popes have made a concerted effort to name cardinals from all parts of the world. It is normally done by identifying the largest and most influential cities in various countries and naming the archbishops of those cities to be cardinals. Pope Francis has also named cardinals from smaller cities and countries around the world.

The bishop of Rome also selects cardinals based on the qualities of the individual person. He selects those he thinks would be the best possible advisors, and who have the right gifts and perspective to vote in a potential conclave to elect a new pope.

Being a cardinal is not a full-time position, it is an additional responsibility given to a bishop. Those named to the College of Cardinals continue the responsibilities they held prior to their elevation. Of note, only those cardinals who are under the age of eighty are eligible to vote in a potential papal conclave.

The Code of Canon Law (Church Law) #351 gives us the process by which a cardinal is created: "Those to be *promoted Cardinals* are *men freely selected* by the *Roman Pontiff*, who are at least in the *order* of *priesthood* and are *truly outstanding* in *doctrine*, *virtue*, *piety* and *prudence* in *practical matters*; those who are not already *Bishops* must *receive episcopal consecration*."

What this canon means is technically, any priest, or even a layman, who is free to be ordained a priest (not married and in good standing with the Catholic church), can be named a cardinal. But before being able to be elevated to the College of Cardinals, anyone who is not already a bishop would need to be ordained a bishop. In reality, virtually all cardinals named these days will already be a bishop.

You can recognize a cardinal by the official color of their office: it is scarlet, a bright shade of red. When new cardinals are given their scarlet biretta (a square hat with three horns on the top), they are reminded the color scarlet signifies their readiness to shed their blood for the faith. They will also wear a scarlet zucchetto (skull-cap) and a scarlet cassock, rather than the fuchsia worn by bishops.

The ceremony for elevating bishops to the College of Cardinals is called a Consistory (meaning "to stand with"). It is the name given to any meeting of the College of Cardinals. The ceremony occurs in the context of a liturgy of the Word and is held at St. Peter's Basilica.

Those who have been selected to be cardinals are called forward by the pope, they make a profession of faith, and then the Holy Father gives each of them a scarlet biretta and a ring, which serve as symbols of their new office. These men are already bishops, so this is not an ordination rite. The next day the entire College of Cardinals concelebrates a Mass with the Holy Father.

In formal correspondence and conversation, cardinals are referred to as "*Your Eminence.*" The proper way of referring to a cardinal by name is to place the title "*Cardinal*" in between their first and last names. Informally, you would say "cardinal" and then his last name.

The College of Cardinals has a long history of papal service. Individually they tend to be highly influential in church affairs; collectively they have the primary responsibility of electing a new pope.

THE ORDER OF CHRISTIAN FUNERALS

The church celebrates the funeral rites in order to offer praise and thanksgiving to God for the gift of life of their loved one who has returned to God the Father in heaven. The celebration of the Funeral Mass, which is actually the memorial of Christ's death and resurrection, is the principal ritual of the Christian funeral. "At the death of a Christian, whose life of faith was begun in the waters of baptism and strengthened at the Eucharistic table, the Church intercedes on behalf of the deceased because of its confident belief that death is not the end nor does it break the bonds forged in life" (*Order of Christian Funerals OCF, #4).*

When a loved one has died, the church celebrates the *Order of Christian Funerals,* which consists of a number of rituals divided into several stations. These form a time of prayer for the families and friends of the deceased. These rituals include the Vigil for the Deceased, the Funeral Liturgy, and the Rite of Committal. The Church also provides a number of *prayers* for the faithful to offer both to accompany the dying of a loved one and to strengthen our faith upon their death.

The Vigil for the Deceased is the official prayer of the Church. It follows the structure of a Liturgy of the Word, consisting of scripture readings, a brief homily, intercessions, and prayers. The focus of the vigil is on the Word of God as the family experiences death and their subsequent grief. The vigil also provides family and friends the opportunity to offer eulogies using their own words to speak about their loved one. The rosary, which is devotion, can be prayed during the hours of visitation, but it is not meant to replace the vigil liturgy of the church.

The funeral liturgy is the heart of the celebration. "At the funeral liturgy the community gathers with the family and friends of the deceased to give praise and thanks to God for Christ's victory over sin and death, to commend the deceased to God's tender mercy and compassion, and to seek strength in the proclamation of the paschal mystery" (*OCF, # 129*). The Funeral Mass is full of symbols, which include the Easter candle, Holy Water, incense, a white garment, and the Book of the Gospel.

The Funeral Mass is structured much like a normal Sunday Mass with the elements of the Introductory Rites helping all present to recall our Baptism. The casket is blessed with holy water reminding the community of the saving waters of Baptism. The casket is clothed with a white garment, called the pall, in remembrance of the white garment worn during the baptism ritual, showing the dignity of the person. The Easter candle is placed near the altar symbolizing the undying presence of Christ among his people. Incense is used during the funeral rite as a sign of honor to the body of the deceased, which became a temple of the Holy Spirit. It is also a sign of the community's prayers for the deceased rising to God as a sign of farewell. The Book of the Gospel is placed on the coffin as a sign that Christians live by the Word of God and that fidelity to that Word leads to eternal life. The celebrant will wear a white chasuble to express Christian hope in the resurrection.

The Liturgy of the Word is an essential element of the celebration since "The readings proclaim the Paschal Mystery, the remembrance of the dead, convey the hope of being gathered together again in God's kingdom, and encourage the witness of Christian life" (OCF, #137). Mass continues with the Liturgy of the Eucharist until after the reception of Holy Communion. The final section of the Mass contains the prayer of Final Commendation and the Song of Farewell. This rite is an act of respect for those who have been entrusted to God. It also acknowledges the reality of separation and affirms that the community and the deceased share the same destiny, which is resurrection on the last day.

The conclusion of the funeral liturgy occurs as a procession to the place of burial. It really mirrors our pilgrimage to God's holy kingdom, which is a place of rest, light, and peace, known as the eternal Jerusalem. The Rite of Committal draws to a close the Funeral Rites of the Catholic Church. The rite can occur at the gravesite, the tomb, or crematorium. These brief prayers show the caring for the body of the loved one. The Rite of Committal "is an expression of the communion that exists between the Church on earth and the Church in heaven" (OCF, #206).

The sadness of death should give way to the promise of immortality. In the celebration of the Order of Christian Funerals, the Catholic Church intercedes on behalf of the deceased because of its confident belief that death is not the end. The Church also ministers to the sorrowing and consoles them in the funeral rites with the comforting Word of God and the celebration of Holy Mass.

THE RITES OF ACCEPTANCE AND WELCOME

The Rite of Acceptance into the Order of Catechumens/Rite of Welcome is a liturgical rite, marking the beginning of the catechumenate process in the Rite of Christian Initiation of Adults (RCIA). In this liturgical rite, the person expresses and the Church accepts their intention to respond to God's call to follow the way of Christ.

The Rite of Acceptance into the Order of Catechumens (Rite of Acceptance) is the first public ritual in the RCIA process. In this rite, a change of identity takes place for the individuals involved: those previously known as inquirers become catechumens. An inquirer is a person who is thinking about becoming acquainted with the Roman Catholic Church. Inquirers with the help of the RCIA team reflect on their own life story and see all the connections it has to the gospel message of Jesus Christ. Throughout this process, the inquirer discerns if they truly desire to become Catholic at this time.

Once the person decides they are ready to commit to becoming Catholic, they are officially welcomed by the Church as disciples. They become members of the church, but not yet full members. This total initiation process will occur on Holy Saturday when they are baptized, confirmed, and receive the Holy Eucharist for the first time.

The Rite of Acceptance into the Order of Catechumens occurs following the opening prayer. During the rite, the inquirer stands in the middle of the parish community and states that he or she wants to become a baptized member of the Catholic Church. The parish assembly affirms this desire and the inquirer becomes a Catechumen.

In the first section of the Rite of Acceptance into the Order of Catechumens, the celebrant receives the candidates. He does this by inviting all the inquirers to come forward. Each person has their name called out and they then respond, "Present." Next, the celebrant asks each one of them individually, "What do you ask of God's Church?" The person responds, "Faith." The celebrant continues, "What does faith offer you?" The person says, "Eternal life."

The celebrant then tells the candidates about the importance of discipleship and the need to align their minds to the mind of Jesus Christ. He says, "You must strive to pattern your life on the teachings of the Gospel and so to love the Lord your God and your neighbor" (RCIA, #52 C). He concludes the section called "The Candidates' First Acceptance of the Gospel" with this question: "Is each of you ready to accept these teachings of the Gospel?" They answer, "I am."

The next part of the rite involves the sponsors and the entire assembly. Each of us has a role to play in the candidates' formation since we are all part of the family of God. That's why he asks us, "Are you ready to help these candidates find and follow Christ?" All present respond, "We are." The celebrant then thanks God for calling the inquirers and for their response.

The signing of the candidates with the cross occurs next. This represents their new way of life. As part of the rite, the inquirers are literally marked with the cross of Christ and claimed as God's own. They are signed on the forehead, so they may know and follow Christ; signed on their ears, so they may hear the voice of the Lord; signed on their eyes, so they may see the glory of God; signed on their lips, so they may respond to the Word of God; signed on their heart, so that Christ may dwell there by faith; signed on their shoulders, so they may bear the gentle yoke of Christ; signed on their hands, so that Christ may be known in the work they do; and also signed on their feet, so they may walk in the way of Christ.

Following the signing, there are intercessions for the Catechumens. Finally, a prayer is prayed over all the Catechumens. Normally this rite is celebrated at a Sunday Mass, which allows the entire Christian community to take an active part in the celebration. While there are no specific Sundays set aside to celebrate this rite, Sundays in ordinary time are excellent choices because of their emphasis on themes of discipleship.

As with the other rites associate with RCIA, every effort is made to show a clear distinction between those unbaptized persons who are seeking full Christian initiation, and those persons already baptized—usually in another Christian denomination—who are seeking reception into the full communion of the Catholic Church.

The Structure of the Rite of Welcome is similar to the Rite of Acceptance. The main difference is there is more freedom given for personal witness of those baptized in another Christian faith in the opening dialogue, then there is in the Rite of Acceptance.

The initiation of adults into the Catholic faith is a gradual process and takes place within the parish community. It is a journey, marked by a number of steps. The Rite of Acceptance into the Order of Catechumens/Rite of Welcome is the first of those liturgical steps,

THE SCRUTINIES

The Second Vatican Council called for the restoration of the adult catechumenate, which really is an extended process of Christian formation for those preparing to enter into the Christian faith. In 1974, the Holy See promulgated the Rite of Christian Initiation of Adults (RCIA). This is a series of rites that serve as part of the preparation for the initiation sacraments of Baptism, Confirmation, and the Eucharist.

The three initiation sacraments normally take place during the celebration of the Easter Vigil. During Lent, we first celebrate a series of preparatory rites as prescribed as part of the Rite of Christian Initiation of Adults. Three of these preparatory rites are the three scrutinies, which occur on the third, fourth, and fifth Sundays of Lent.

The Scrutinies are rites of self-searching and repentance. The liturgical ritual book associated with RCIA teaches us, "The scrutinies are meant to uncover, then heal all that is weak, defective or sinful in the hearts of the Elect (those preparing for the initiation sacraments); to bring out, then strengthen, all that is upright, strong and good. For the scrutinies are celebrated in order to deliver the elect from the power of sin and Satan, to protect them against temptation, and to give them strength in Christ, who is the way, the truth and the life. These rites, therefore, should complete the conversion of the elect and deepen their resolve to hold fast to Christ and to carry out their decision to love God above all" (Rite of Christian Initiation of Adults, #141).

These liturgical rites are celebrated during a Sunday Mass. The purpose of including these rites during a Sunday Liturgy is twofold: they remind the entire faith community they have a role in supporting the elect and to realize that conversion happens not just during

Lent but each and every day, as a communal commitment not just a personal one. These rites include prayers of intercession and the laying on of hands so that the Holy Spirit may be invoked and the spirit of evil cast out. Whenever we celebrate the scrutinies, Holy Mother Church instructs us to proclaim the gospel readings from the Cycle A set of readings. These gospels focus on the woman at the well from Samaria, the man born blind, and the raising of Lazarus. All of these gospel readings focus on new life in Christ.

The entire Church prays the scrutinies during the holy season of Lent as a way to support and actually encourage a spirit of repentance among those who seek the Sacrament of Baptism during the Easter Vigil. The Constitution of the Sacred Liturgy (CSL) teaches, "The season of Lent has a twofold character: primarily by recalling or preparing for baptism and by penance, it disposes the faithful, who more diligently hear the word of God and devote themselves to prayer, to celebrate the paschal mystery (the life, death, and resurrection of Jesus)" (CSL, #109).

The scrutinies are not something new to the Catholic Church; they were celebrated during the fourth and fifth century by St. Ambrose and St. Augustine. These rites marked the spiritual progress of the Catechumens. To help with that progress, the moral preparation of Catechumens included prayers of exorcism, to drive out the spirit of evil, which kept them from embracing Christ as their light.

Their purpose examines the candidates' spiritual readiness. Scrutinies offer the Catechumens the support they need to approach the waters of the baptismal font. For the majority of parishioners who are already baptized, these Lenten scrutinies invite us to embrace that same spirit of self-searching and repentance. During Lent as the Catechumens are scrutinized, we too should renew our commitment to repentance. The scrutinies remind us of the seriousness of our Christian life and inspire us to turn from evil and pursue good. They enliven our recommitment to Christ at Easter.

Throughout the celebration of the scrutinies, we experience the beauty and power of the rites in the prayers prayed. During the first Scrutiny, the priest prays, "Grant that these your catechumens, who like the woman of Samaria, thirst for living water, may turn to the

Lord as they hear his word and acknowledge the sins and weaknesses that weigh them down"(RCIA, #154). On the second Scrutiny we hear, "Father of mercy, you led the man born blind to the kingdom of light through the gift of faith in your Son" (RCIA, #168). In the exorcism prayer for the third Scrutiny the celebrant prays, "Lord Jesus, by raising Lazarus from the dead you showed that you came that we might have life and have it more abundantly. Free from the grasp of death those who await your life-giving sacraments and deliver them from the spirit of corruption" (RCIA, #175).

Celebrating the scrutinies is not only part of the journey of the catechumens (elect) during Lent; it is also part of our journey. All of us are called to examine our lives so we may live with the spirit of the gospel and receive new strength on our spiritual journey.

About the Author

Charlie Dispenzieri, M.A.P.T., received his Master of Arts in Pastoral Theology with an emphasis in liturgy from St. Mary of the Woods College in Terre Haute, Indiana. He currently serves as the Director of Worship for St. Elizabeth Seton Catholic Church in Carmel, Indiana. Charlie regularly teaches courses in liturgy and sacraments in the deacon formation programs for St. Meinrad School of Theology and for the Diocese of Lafayette in Indiana, in addition to teaching Ecclesial Lay Ministry classes for church ministers. Charlie is also an adjunct professor at the University of Dayton where he instructs liturgy, sacraments, Scripture, and catechesis courses in The Virtual Learning Community for Faith Formation (VLCFF) program. His liturgical ministry experience spans over three decades in the areas of liturgy, liturgical catechesis, and music. He has authored over 150 articles on liturgy and sacraments; has presented workshops on the liturgical year, liturgical ministry, liturgy and sacraments and music; and has facilitated parish retreats. Charlie is a fourth-degree knight in the Knights of Columbus where he serves as the state sacristan.